You Are Not Alone

Stories from the front lines of womanhood

For Erin,
With all my love
Leah Carey

An autobiography in 10 voices

Conceived and edited by

Leah Carey

This book is dedicated to all those who created a tipping point in the conversation about gender equality in our culture. By speaking about your experiences and a new vision for the future, you have catalyzed a healthier conversation than we've ever been able to have before. Thank you.

Printed in the United States of America

First Printing, 2014

ISBN 0-69228-561-x

Leah Carey, LLC
www.LeahCarey.com

For bulk purchasing and other special sales of this book, contact Sales@LeahCarey.com.

To book Leah Carey as a keynote speaker for your next event, contact YouAreNotAlone@LeahCarey.com

CONTENTS

#

#YesAllWomen
because awareness and fear of rape is just a normal part of being a woman. Like breathing and eating.

@TheRyPepper

CHAPTER 1

How often?

How often have you had to...

...cross the street to avoid the guys who were walking toward you, laughing a little too loud?

...hold your keys between your fingers, with the points out, while walking at night in case someone attacks you?

...be nervous about turning down a man's advances, lest he get upset and turn aggressive?

...ask a man to go car shopping with you so you wouldn't be taken advantage of?

...pretend not to know an answer so someone won't find you threatening?

For many of us, these are the background stories of our lives. They are habitual things we do, often without even thinking about them, because we've been acclimatized to fear, to doubting ourselves, and to thinking of ourselves as the "weaker sex". They are the story of being a woman in today's society. And while each one of us lives them in her own way each day, we rarely talk about it. It's just normal life, so what is there to talk about?

CHAPTER 2

War on Womanhood

When I was 10 years old, I heard a lot about good posture. My ballet teacher talked about it all the time. So did my mom. But most of all, I heard it from my chiropractor who was treating me for scoliosis. Good posture was a necessity if I didn't want to end up wearing a back brace.

I practiced moving my shoulders down and back and imagining that a string was pulling me up from the top of my head. I wasn't perfect at it, but the idea of that back brace gave me a lot of motivation to keep trying.

One day a boy in my class sidled up to me and said, "Why are you sticking out your chest. Do you want us all to stare at your boobs?"

I was shattered. I barely had "boobs" to speak of. It had never occurred to me that, even if I did have them, anyone would want to look at them.

That very day I started slouching and wearing baggy clothes. I did anything I could to prevent *anyone* from thinking I was putting myself – or my body – on display.

It was that day, at 10 years old, and without even knowing it, that I went to war with my own womanhood.

We live in a media culture that shows us highly sexualized images of women. It sells us clothing that is either tight and sexy or frumpy – there is hardly an in-between. It tells us that if we have lines on our faces or a jiggle in our thighs we are not desirable.

And when we internalize those ideas – that we must have a certain body type and dress a certain way to be acceptable – we are shamed for being too provocative. Then the message gets even more twisted by telling us that boys can't control themselves around us, thus putting the responsibility for male behavior squarely on female shoulders.

There is a lot of talk in the media about political and religious organizations perpetuating a "war on women." But it doesn't require a political party or a religious group to start a "war on women."

Here is the sad truth: We don't need them to do it for us. We are already doing it to ourselves.

They are just saying out loud what we're already saying to ourselves. What we are unwittingly saying to our daughters through how we speak about ourselves and about other women. What we are unknowingly teaching our sons about women through the behavior that we accept from the men in our world.

Through the reflections in this book, I hope we can bring a new awareness to how we treat ourselves and others.

In sharing our stories, we see that we are not alone in believing what others have told us...and what we have told ourselves.

Perhaps we can begin the healing process and learn a new way of being that is based in the belief that we are okay exactly the way we are.

Perhaps we can do better for the next generation.

CHAPTER 3

The day Twitter exploded

On May 23, 2014, a young man named Elliot Rodger uploaded a video to YouTube titled "Elliot Rodger's Retribution" and emailed what has been described as a 140-page "manifesto" titled "My Twisted World."

Taken together, these two documents offer a glimpse into the mind of a disturbed young man who believed that women are incapable of rational thought and "haven't evolved from animal-like thinking." He blamed his misery in life on the fact that women refused to be intimate with him. He vowed to punish them for that refusal.

He then went on a shooting spree, killing six people, injuring 13 more, before finally committing suicide in Isla Vista, California, near the campus of University of California, Santa Barbara.

Rodger's words were a very visible demonstration of why so many women develop a generalized fear of men – it's impossible to differentiate the "safe" men from the attackers by looks alone. Prior to May 23, if you had gathered ten photos of young men, including one of Elliot Rodger, there would have been no reason to pick his out as the one who was going to turn into a killer.

The violence and sense of male sexual entitlement demonstrated in his words struck a nerve with women across the globe. They took to Twitter.com, the short-form social media site, using the hashtag #YesAllWomen.

There are conflicting reports about how the #YesAllWomen hashtag was initiated, but this much is certain: it quickly caught fire. According to an article on Mashable.com published on May 26, "#YesAllWomen — which didn't exist before May 24 — has been attached to 1.2 million tweets."

In their tweets, women took the opportunity to describe - in 140 characters or less - their experiences of harassment, discrimination, assault, sexism, and violence on an emotional, physical, and sexual level.

The act of women giving voice to their experiences was enough to incite a small, but vocal, group to violent words and the threat of violent action. Amongst these "trolls[1]" were men who threatened rape and murder against the women who were using Twitter to share their feelings. They attacked women's right to speak, to walk down the street, and to choose their own sexual partners.

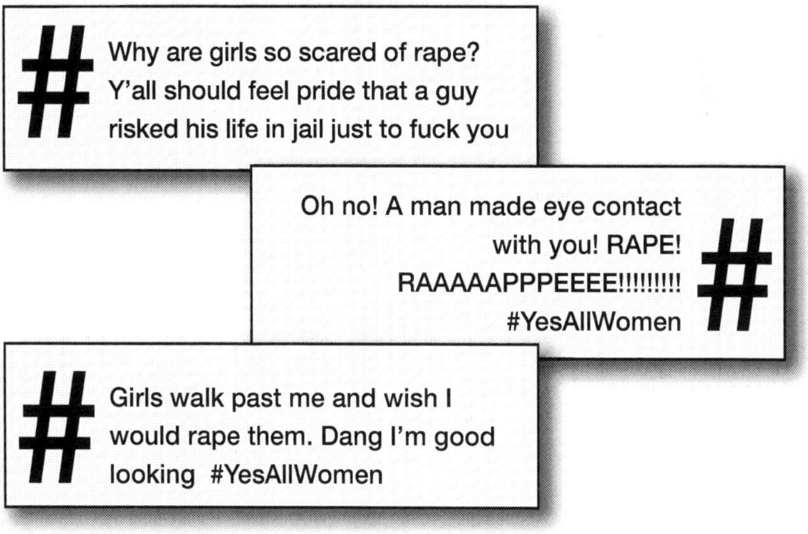

[1] A Twitter "troll" is a person who intentionally harasses other users by posting inflammatory or violent messages about them.

It quickly became a reflection of what every woman has experienced at some point when walking alone at night. I won't honor these trolls by attaching their usernames to their words. But I think it is important to acknowledge some of the ugly and thoughtless language they use to threaten and intimidate women. Whether it is spoken blatantly online or it courses under the surface of an interaction on the street, this is a part of what women face daily. It exists as part of our consciousness each time we walk out the front door.

I discovered the #YesAllWomen phenomenon about three days after it started, and the posts were still flying fast and furious. When I put up my own posts announcing that I was organizing a writing workshop inspired by the Twitter conversation (more on that in a moment), I, too, received many of those hateful responses.

One of the original *You Are Not Alone* writers – I'll call her Laura – felt so threatened by the violent words in social media that she chose to withdraw from the group early. She feared that, by participating in this workshop, she would be putting herself and her daughter in danger. Here is a portion of the email she sent me explaining her withdrawal from the group:

> *I am frightened of these men, pouring out of the woodwork who are happy to proclaim their right to be violent in a PUBLIC FORUM like Twitter. No wonder they feel it is okay to rape in dark alleys, they do it right there in public.*

She is not alone in her fear. During the height of the Twitter conversation, there were astonishing threats of violence against the women who were sharing their stories.

Other women in the *You Are Not Alone* group of writers also struggled with this dilemma: How do we keep our children safe and teach them to offer and expect respect when there is so little respect in evidence in our society?

In the face of this harassment, however, there were also many men who recognized the importance of what was going on and wrote supportive tweets like this one:

> \#
>
> "Tired" of **#YesAllWomen**? Take any random tweet from a woman with this hashtag and read the disgusting replies. Repeat until you understand.
>
> *@billnordwall*

Hashtag activism

When the #YesAllWomen conversation started on Twitter, some men felt like they were being vilified for their gender. They used the hashtag #NotAllMen to point out that not all men are attackers. Unfortunately they did it using aggressive and sometimes violent language.

Another group of men started the hashtag #AllMenCan, pointing out that all men can make a positive difference in the world through how they treat women.

There was also a group of women who used the #YesAllWomen tag to harass and make fun of other women for being too sensitive, paranoid, or hysterical.

Both men *and* women participated in the hashtag #YesAllWomenJokes, displaying some truly demented and offensive "humor" at the expense of women.

The various hashtags and social issues are highlighting a need for a broad conversation that is as much about respect as it is about gender. The need for respect crosses all lines: gender, race, age, class, etc.

Not an isolated incident

The Isla Vista shooting is not an isolated event. We live in a culture that systematically calls women's safety and rights into question. Within just one month before and after the shootings, there were several other events in the United States, often thought of as *the most free nation on earth*, that serve as a commentary on how women are viewed in our society.

In May 2014, a scandal caught fire at some of the country's most esteemed colleges and universities when 55 schools were placed under federal investigation for their handling of sexual violence and harassment complaints. At one school that was prominently featured in news reports, a student found responsible for raping a woman was punished with a five-page book report.

On June 30, 2014, the United States Supreme Court ruled in the case of Burwell v. Hobby Lobby Stores, Inc., that a "closely-held corporation" could refuse to provide female employees with no-cost access to certain types of birth control based on the company's religious views. According to their own press material, the "closely held corporation" of Hobby Lobby employs over 18,000 people and has over $2 billion in annual revenues. With the Hobby Lobby decision, Social media again went into overdrive, decrying a for-profit company's right to make decisions about their female employees' health care.

> # **#YesAllWomen**
> because we can't even use the hashtag without death threats.
> *@kimgirvanx*

According to the Guttmacher Institute, in the first half of 2014 alone, United States legislators have put forward 468 bills designed to regulate women's bodies. In the same period, there have been *zero* bills designed to regulate men's bodies.

But this isn't just about man-on-woman violence or a group of "old white men" trying to legislate women's bodies. We attack each other as women on a regular basis too, and you'll read some of those stories in this book.

Why this book? Why now?

You may be asking yourself – if the Twitter conversation was so intense, why is this book necessary?

There are a few reasons...

First, when Twitter exploded on May 25, 2014, the issues of harassment, assault, and violence against women came to the forefront of the nation's consciousness when a critical mass of voices spoke at the same time. The actions of one young man provided the spark that ignited fuel that has been building for decades – even centuries. It is a conversation that has happened amongst women in hushed tones for a very long time. But far too often, women have been told they were being "overly sensitive" or "hysterical" or "paranoid" when they shared their experiences. With the advent of social media, it is no longer each woman for herself. Thanks to conversations like #YesAllWomen, a critical mass of voices has been raised and can now be widely acknowledged, heard, and shared, rather than silenced and shamed. It is thanks to many individuals, like the *You Are Not Alone* writers, that the conversation continues.

Second, there is a limit to what can be expressed in a single 140-character tweet. The stories in this book expand on the themes seen in the online conversation, providing context and repercussions that can't be detailed in a single tweet.

Third, research shows that when we share our stories in a supportive group setting and then with a wider audience, two things happen: we find relief from the fear and shame that have plagued us as a result of our experiences; and we help others to find relief from their fear and shame because, in hearing their experiences mirrored back to them, they know that they are not alone.[2]

Finally, it's important to reiterate that hostile and degrading be-

---

[2] In 2005 I was invited to write an article for the Journal of Cancer Education, a peer-reviewed medical journal of the American and European Journals of Cancer Education on this subject. You can find the article at www.LeahCarey.com. The full reference information is:

Bosom Buddies: a practical model of expressive disclosure, Journal of Cancer Education. 2005 Winter;20(4):251-5.

havior toward women doesn't come solely from men. As you will see in multiple pieces of writing throughout this book, it is also an issue amongst women. We have internalized so many of the lessons of our culture that we use them against ourselves and each other.

This is not just a man vs. woman problem. It is a larger systemic cultural and social issue to which we all contribute. Both men and women are necessary in the search for a solution.

This is not a man vs. woman book. It is, I hope, part of a larger conversation that explores where we are now – both the good and the bad. The *You Are Not Alone* writers stand in as the "everywoman," sharing their experiences in every aspect of their lives so we can look at the issues from a real-life perspective. Studies and statistics are important, but this conversation is about so much more. These stories are personal, opening the door to an exploration beyond the researchers and sociologists, and bringing it into our living rooms, bedrooms, and workrooms. In this way we can see more clearly where and how things need to change.

> #
>
> Because no one is entitled to my body, thoughts or happiness but me. **#YesAllWomen**
>
> *@Zombies_queen*

Why this book?

Because in 2009, the Dalai Lama said, "The world will be saved by the Western woman."

Our time has come.

CHAPTER 4

Impossible expectations

Not all men are attackers. Not all women are saints. At this juncture, it's important to recognize one key factor: the harassment and assault that women experience at the hands of *some* men happen within a larger context.

We live in a society that makes a game out of disrespecting each other. Boys grow up trying to think up bigger and badder "Yo Mama" jokes. Girls grow up learning to evaluate each other based on whether we're wearing the right color foundation or we've "caught" the perfect boyfriend.

Watch any 30-minute sitcom and count the number of times the laugh track is cued by a joke that is made at the expense of another person's dignity.

And while women take a large hit for being ditzy or controlling or bitchy, men don't get off any easier.

Think back to that sitcom again. If there's a married couple at the center of it, you'll almost certainly see a bumbling husband who is constantly messing up, and then being corrected and covered up for by his saintly wife.

Watch any standard set of five television commercials, and you'll see the same storyline play out at least once. Man says or does something stupid; wife rolls her eyes; wife corrects whatever the man has done with the wonder product; and life goes on for the man to mess up another day.

We put impossible demands on men in this society. Look at any summer blockbuster to see our idealized version of what a man is supposed to look and act like. We swoon over the male model and action heroes with six-pack abs, forgetting that they can't develop and maintain that six pack while also excelling at a good-paying job, going to the park with us and the kids, doing the dishes, fixing the car, and maintaining a healthy relationship full of deep communication.

And then, on top of all of that, we want them to be sensitive enough to cry…but not *too much*.

We lump them into a group – *"ugh, men, they just don't get it!"* – and treat them with disrespect, but then expect absolute respect in return.

Something has to give.

Even amongst my mostly open-minded and spiritually-inclined friends on Facebook, it is completely acceptable to bash men in "amusing" images and status updates. Here's one example that recently showed up in my Facebook feed from several different people:

WOMAN'S ASS SIZE STUDY

There is a new study about women and how they feel about their asses. The results were very interesting:

10% **of women think her ass is too skinny**

30% **of women think her ass is too fat**

60% **say they don't care, at least he's her ass.**

I'll admit – I chuckled the first time I saw it. But the second time I saw it, I started thinking...*wait a minute!* If a man replaced the word "ass" with a feminine equivalent and posted it, we would go CRAZY! And rightfully so. So why do we consider it okay to say these things about our male counterparts?

> **#**
>
> **Because my friendship is seen as punishment and a prison sentence instead of a privilege. #YesAllWomen**
>
> *@msshannybear*

We live in an atmosphere of disrespect where it is perfectly acceptable to label people as "the other" and then treat them as less than human. Whether it's people from other cultures or people of the other gender, we dehumanize them in our minds *every day*. And then we're surprised when they act toward us as if *we* were less than human. It is a vicious cycle; and to break that cycle, we must be willing to look at some uncomfortable truths about ourselves.

Some of the tweets using the hashtag #YesAllWomen *do* cross the line into male-bashing. And while that's not a reason to dismiss and ridicule the entire conversation, neither can I fault men who see that and think, "Why should I listen?"

The stories told in the #YesAllWomen conversation are perfect examples of how men disrespect and abuse women; but if we don't begin to change the conversation, the war on womanhood will only be perpetuated. Respect is a two-way street. If we want men to listen to and respect us, we also need to consider how we listen to and respect them.[3]

---

[3] There will be some girls and women for whom this call to respect the men in their lives is inappropriate, even dangerous. Whether she is being abused by a family member or lives in fear of her spouse, learning to listen to and be more respectful of her abuser won't aid the situation because there are larger issues at play. If you need help in leaving an abusive situation, you can find the National Domestic Violence Hotline at www.thehotline.org or 1-800-799-7233.

CHAPTER 5

The creation of this book

I got caught up in the social media conversation because I have a story of abuse, harassment, and fear. In fact, I have a multitude of them – just like most women.

When I first started reading on Twitter, I was filled with rage and sadness. I could barely sit still at work. I wanted to jump out of my skin and scream at anybody who dared come within 10 feet of me.

Unsure what to do, lest I explode, I started conversations with the important women in my life. We shared some of our stories. As we talked, the rage began to drain from my body.

This is the power of telling our stories.

In fact, I've been leading workshops for 10 years around these very principles: writing our stories is healing for us; sharing our stories is healing for others.

I've seen it happen again and again over 10 years of group facilitation: when a woman speaks her truth, her voice changes; her body relaxes; the lines on her face smooth. And, very often, within days or weeks I hear from her, telling me that her life has changed for the better.

I quickly recognized that a space had opened and the group writing process is exactly what was called for: a sharing of stories; a coming together; a sense of sisterhood.

And so, in order to involve women from all over the world, I created a space for them to meet online via the magic of video conferencing. It offered a small group of women a place to explore their personal stories in a deeper way, and then share them with the world.

I publicized the four-week writing workshop on Twitter and other social media, inviting women who were already in the active in the #YesAllWomen conversation. It was my intention to include women of all ages, races, religions, and geography so the conversation could cover the broad range of issues that are faced by women worldwide. Once the invitations went out, it was a first-come, first-served registration process. I was very pleased when women showed up from all over the continental United States, Hawaii, and New Zealand.

> # Because a U.S. woman has more regulations on her reproductive rights than the country has on gun control. **#YesAllWomen**
>
> *@a_mandolin*

For four weeks, the women came together to write, listen, and share. Some of them have writing aspirations. Others found the idea of putting their thoughts down on paper to be *very* daunting. But whether they consider themselves writers or not, they kept showing up.

All of this happened fast. From the inception of the idea, to creating and publicizing the workshop, to writing with the women, to gathering and editing their material for publication was only 12 weeks.

And the result is breathtaking. These women are ready to tell their stories. They are *ready to be heard.*

These are women who are ready to move the conversation forward and move on with their lives.

There are no easy answers here

What you will find in these pages is remarkable not just for its depth and wisdom, but also for the fact that all of it was created in periods of not more than 20 minutes.[4] It is amazing what the heart and mind can express when given even the smallest window.

What you will not find is easy answers. *There are no easy answers* on the topic of women in today's society. You *will* find thoughtful inquiry into difficult subjects.

You will not find condemnation or vilification of an entire gender in this book. Neither will you find glorification of an entire gender.

Told through stories from their own lives, the women in this book are not prone to clichés or pleasant platitudes. They dug within themselves to find wisdom...but they also revealed their own inner conflict about their experiences and their views of the world. They were willing to be vulnerable enough to show parts of themselves that aren't always pretty.

You probably won't agree with everything that is said in these pages. I, as the facilitator and editor, don't agree with everything in these pages. But that's okay. It's okay for us to disagree as long as we can still listen and hear each other. It has become rare to have conversations with respect amongst people who hold differing viewpoints. Too often, conversations on meaningful topics devolve into mudslinging matches that focus on a person's intellect or morals, rather than on substantive subjects. We are so focused on being heard as we argue for our viewpoint that we often forget to listen.

One of the things that makes a workshop like this successful is that the women approach each other with respect. That type of respect is fostered when we focus on understanding how another person feels and why they acted the way they did, rather than focusing on the perceived rightness or wrongness of the action itself.

---

[4] There has been some light editing since the first writing – some pieces have been combined, others have been deconstructed in order to create a cohesive flow for print – but the initial writing periods were only 5, 10, or 20 minutes long.

What you will find in these pages is an attempt to put an individual face on the experience of being a woman – to take it out of the realm of "*they* always do..." and "*they* are..." and put it back into the realm of "this is how *she* felt." In doing that, these women have uncovered some uncomfortable truths and are admitting the places where they, too, have treated others with less than the dignity that they wish for themselves.

We are not faceless members of a group called "women." We are individuals, and we each have a story to share.

I created this workshop in order to create a space for deep listening. What showed up as a result was deep sharing.

> #
>
> **How would you feel if someone did what you were thinking/ doing to your mother or sister? #YesAllWomen**
>
> *@EmmieLou_22*
>
> *Emma Harper*

The workshop sessions opened up meaningful conversations amongst the women involved. And now we are sharing our musings with you, hoping that it will help you to open similar conversations with your friends and neighbors and loved ones. Every person who engages in a thoughtful consideration of these issues contributes to a ripple effect for positive change.

When I facilitate a workshop, there is one thing that always makes my heart flutter... and it happens every time people come together to share their stories. This time it came from 17-year-old Ashley, the youngest of our members and wise beyond her years. As she reflected back on the four weeks we spent together, she wrote the words that make all of this worthwhile for me: "I have learned that I am not alone."

You are not alone. Whatever you have experienced – mental, emotional, physical, or gender abuse from a man, a woman, or yourself – *You. Are. Not. Alone.*

I hope that you will hear those words repeating in your head as you read this book and realize how true they are:

You are not alone.

CHAPTER 6

It's time

The Dalai Lama told us that the world would be saved by the Western woman.

It is time for us to put on our capes and become the superheroes the world needs.

We're not saving the world FROM men. We're not saving the world FOR women.

We're saving the world from our *fear.*

We're saving the world from our *shame.*

We're saving the world from all those times that we didn't speak our truth, and *turned our anger inward on ourselves.*

We're saving the world from all those times that we didn't speak our truth and exploded at innocent bystanders...*many of whom happen to be the men who want to love us.*

We're saving the world by finding peace and respect within ourselves, because it will save the world *for the next generation.*

CHAPTER 7

A note to our male readers

Perhaps you have been given this book by your wife, daughter, mother, or friend. Perhaps she thought that you could learn a bit about how different their life is from yours. Certainly, she thought you would be an ally in making the world a safer, more welcoming place for her to live.

Perhaps you picked this book up on your own because the title caught your attention.

Either way, simply by opening its cover, you've already shown that you are part of the solution. But you may still be asking...why should I care about this discussion?

Here is a bit of my own story that I hope will begin to answer that question for you...

I took the R train from Manhattan to Queens by myself at midnight.

I walked alone after dark through not-great parts of town.

Both things would have terrified my mother if I'd told her at the time, but they were simply a part of the life I lived – I worked nights in the theater and didn't make enough money to live somewhere closer and "safer."

I learned to put on "the face" – the one that says, "I'm cold and mean and you don't want to fuck with me." And they didn't.

But here's the problem – and here's the reason that you, as a man, should care – I didn't know how to turn off "the face."

It's not as easy as turning a light on and off. When we harden the exterior, it's almost impossible to avoid hardening the soft soul underneath.

I didn't know how to let down my guard. I didn't know how to soften and then harden again as necessary, so I stayed in that hardened state throughout my time in the city. I never allowed myself to revel in a feeling of safety and security, even in the quiet moments.

And it's the same, whether in a huge city or a rural town. We protect ourselves with armor of steel against the arrows that have been slung at us – the "slut," the "bitch," the "you would if you loved me," the "you'll never be as pretty as your friend," the "you're too fat to be pretty." And it takes a long time to remove the armor.

So here comes you – the good man, the man who wants to love me, who wants to adore me and appreciate me. You come near, and through my steely gaze I can no longer differentiate your gentle devotions from the manipulations I've heard and seen in others.

I cannot shed the armor in a moment simply because you seem on first glance to be a good guy. Have you ever seen someone remove a suit of armor? It takes a long time, and it happens piece by piece.

Why should you care that men you don't know are abusing,

harassing, and assaulting us? Because in the face of that treatment, we make difficult choices – and one of them is often to close ourselves off. It makes it harder for YOU to get close…even though you may be the one we have been searching for, yearning for, dreaming about for years. Even though you may be the one who makes us feel truly safe.

It's not true that "nice guys" aren't attractive to us. But there are a lot of men who walk around claiming very loudly that they are "nice guys" and then tearing us to shreds through their words or deeds.

So why should you care? Because we want to know you, but first we need to know safety. And until we trust in our safety, we can't open our hearts to truly know you.

That is why this is your fight as much as it is ours. That is why you should care.

Thank you for standing with us, and with all of the women whom you love and respect.

> #
>
> Started reading the **#YesAllWomen** tweets because I've got a daughter, but now I see I should be reading them because I've got two sons.
>
> *@awdubreuil*

#YesAllWomen

Because almost EVERY woman I know (including myself) has been the victim of sexual harassment or a violent sex crime. Or both.

@martinoxon

CHAPTER 8

Meet the *You Are Not Alone* writers

Anne Howe

I am 53, and I have worked in arts, education, and community development for more than 20 years. I have lived in four states and two foreign countries, and now make my home in Vermont. Having cared for others as a girlfriend, wife, mother and caregiver for most of my adult life, I'm feeling a need to take time for myself and have been craving deeper connections with other women.

I have long struggled to trust my voice, and I welcomed this opportunity to challenge myself to share in a supportive and nonjudgmental forum. I have written a lot in my work and academic career, but rarely have allowed myself the time and space to write about myself, which is both frightening and freeing.

Anne has chosen to use a pseudonym in order to protect her privacy.

Ashley Freeman

I am a 17-year-old senior at a small Southern California charter school. I enjoy juggling, unicycling, and swinging on trapezes in the Great Y Circus, playing video games, running, and petting my cat. I am a strong advocate for LGBT Rights and the Feminist Movement, and actively participate in my high school's Pride Club. I plan to study Mechanical Engineering, and I want to inspire other young girls to take an interest in STEM (science, technology, engineering and math) fields.

Crysti Caro

I am a disabled lawyer who now spends time championing the working mother's right to be ambitious without guilt. I speak about the need for daycare reform to match the modern working world.

I need feminism and hashtags such as #YesAllWomen as much at 39 as many young girls do. Having been raised in the patriarchal ideologies of the southern United States, I was previously enmeshed in educational, religious, and political systems that preached that women are pretty objects to be taken care of by men, because they know so much more about all things God and State.

I am eternally grateful to have left that ultra-conservative mindset and to have found the brave women who speak out on Twitter about why we need feminism. I am now even more determined to thoroughly unravel my roots in patriarchy for the sake of educating my three sons.

Elizabeth Devine

I am 27 years old and pursuing a degree in engineering technology. I was first published at 17 years old in an anthology called *Oh Georgia, Too!* I have been a pro-style wrestler, a professional glamour model, and a well-respected dominatrix. I self-published an (unpolished) poetry anthology on smashwords called *What Makes a Mean Girl* and will soon publish its sequel *What Makes a Man-Eater.* You can find me online at www.ElizaDivine.com.

Despite learning early in life that my body was not my own, my time in the world of professional domination taught me that all fantasies can be lived in a safe, sane, and consensual manner with willing participants. Now retired from professional BDSM, I focus the majority of my energy on my writing, on short films, and various forms of outreach and education.

Grace Williams

I am 48 years old and have spent the last 13 years living in Hawaii. I have a background in education as well as experience working in the not-for-profit development, theater, and travel and tourism industries. From the east coast and a resident of New York City for 18 years, I have traveled the world, for the most part alone.

Grace has chosen to use a pseudonym in order to protect her privacy.

Leah Carey

In addition to organizing and facilitating writing workshops, I am also a writer. Because I often facilitate workshops on subjects that I don't have personal experience with, I don't usually write with the participants. However, the subject of #YesAllWomen and womanhood is one that is very close to my heart, and that I spend a lot of time thinking about. In this compilation, I have included some of my own pieces of writing. Some of these were written during the workshop, using the same prompts I gave the women and others were written in the past couple years as part of my blog, *The Miracle Journal* (www.TheMiracleJournal.com).

Leah Niblett

As an anthropologist, the study of culture has always been an integral part of my life. Taking the time to respond to and participate in the pivotal moments in my own culture is truly important. I have always been a writer of sorts. Aside from academic papers and publications, my major medium has been through journaling. This experience has allowed me to explore my creative side once more and helped me define my writer's voice.

Aside from writing, I rescue retired racing greyhounds and volunteer in a clinic for injured and ill birds of prey to enable them to be released in the wild. In my spare time I knit, make jam and pickles, and spend as much time as I can at the beach. I am 32 and live in South Carolina.

In an odd twist of fate, instead of having two Susans or Julies in the group, we had two Leahs! In order to differentiate our writing throughout the book, Leah Niblett will appear as "Leah N." and Leah Carey will appear as "Leah C."

Mercedes Vasquez

My story is really just beginning. I stand here at 23 years of age, still trying to learn as much as I can about the world around me. I am from the Los Angeles area and am currently earning my doctorate in forensic psychology, having previously graduated with a degree in Anthropology, English, and Applied Psychology from University of California, Santa Barbara. Painting, creative writing, exploring new places and ideas, and community involvement are other passions of mine. I am also a certified dog trainer and love going on hikes with my own wonderful pup, Mandy Clementine.

My life as a woman of color and my life as a sister are what have inspired me to work on this project. My younger sister has always been a motivator for me, and it is my aspiration to be a figure of inspiration and motivation for her. In addition, I am a proud sister of Sigma Theta Psi Multicultural Sorority. I am being inspired and motivated every day by the lifelong connections I have made with this sisterhood. My writings are therefore dedicated to the many different kinds of sisters who have come into my life.

Rachel Davita Harris

This work is very close to my heart. Like so many women, as I grew up in Miami, Florida, I experienced the scarring effects of objectification at a young age. Writing my own story, for myself, allowed me to heal and encounter my own voice. Afterwards, I led women's memoir writing groups. As I work now, at 27 years old, to stand up on my own two feet in this world, I hope that over time, helping women share their stories will become the center of my own life's work. I encourage everyone to read our words from the space inside of you that knows how to feel.

Sabrinna Valisce

I trained in Ballet and then discovered Contemporary dance and fell in love with it. I trained full-time. I always knew I wanted to be a dancer, and for a short time I was. I was hit by a car and spent three years learning to walk again. The emotional journey felt like climbing many mountains: first accepting what had happened, then accepting what that meant, then finding a new way through and overcoming others' prejudices and judgments. I went into choreography and teaching, working with dancers and circus performers. Many times, I've had to prove myself worthy of creating choreography despite having some physical limitations. I'm now looking at entering a new area of work, and fingers crossed, I'll be working with tarot, astrology and spiritual practices within the year. I still love choreography and the performing arts and would like to work on passion projects from here on in. I live in New Zealand.

I'm choosing to use my name and my photo because being visible and heard is an area I'm working on in my personal life. It's challenging because part of it is owning my own views and knowing my worldview will not please everyone, and that's okay.

#YesAllWomen Twitter participants

Throughout the book, you'll find **#YesAllWomen** quotes from the Twitter conversation. These are the people who built this conversation from a small spark into a revolution.

Each of the tweets are quoted with the permission of the author. Due to the nature of Twitter, it's not always possible to know who the first person was to make a particular post. In each case, I reached out to the person who I first saw posting the words.

> #
> **I ignore guys when they hit on me. Not because I'm a bitch, but because it makes me uncomfortable. #YesAllWomen**
>
> *@bluecollarbetty*

To aid people who are not familiar with the conventions of Twitter, spelling and punctuation in the quoted tweets have been corrected to improve readability. The words have not been changed.

CHAPTER 9

Defining womanhood

Entire industries are built around standards of womanhood – whether it's makeup and hair products or laundry detergent, companies target women based on age-old gender roles. Much has changed in the last few decades, but many of the old stereotypes still remain.

As the *You Are Not Alone* writers came together for the first time, it seemed important to lay a foundation for exactly what we'd be talking about. I asked them: What is womanhood? What does it mean to you?

by **Rachel**

Womanhood is a sliver of something I once found inside myself but usually forget.
Shining.
Powerful.
Blue.

Some women can make me recall this deep femininity.
This standing up.
Speaking free.

Joy radiating from our pores.

I catch it for a second, what it really means to speak out loud.
And then it dips back into the sea.

by **Anne**

Loving
Opening

by **Sabrinna**

Sit still,
knees together,
be polite,
smile,
don't boast,
be friendly…but not too friendly,
dress modestly,
be safe,
stay safe,
don't take risks ...

by **Anne**

Conflicted
Alone

by **Grace**

What is womanhood?
Is it a prescribed role that one must meet?

Where we must be nurturing?
Have children?
Be sisters with other women?

I call myself a feminist.
But, truly, I wish just to call myself human.
I wish that there were no such thing as misogyny or in-equality.

But, there is.

I wish I didn't have expectations of myself and others. But I still do.

by **Anne**

Trying to please everyone
Not good enough

by **Rachel**

Yesterday, standing in front of my kitchen stove, mixing pancakes, I thought: the world is beyond me (it's also in me, I think now). But either way, it has its ways, the world has its ways.

by **Anne**

Confusing
Sharing

by **Sabrinna**

Womanhood is negotiating the myths and the realities of life.

It is upholding falsehoods
like the myth of the
great male protector

While never having experienced
male protection,
even when you needed it the most.

Womanhood is negotiating
other peoples' expectations
and why I'm not living up to them.

Why are you single? Why aren't you a mother?

Womanhood is a class. It's been called second-class,
the sex-class and
the other sex.

by **Anne**

Warmth
Fragile

by **Mercedes**

The word "womanhood" can bring up many different kinds of emotions. Depending on who you ask, you will receive very different answers, not just in context but in the tone they inspire. This is not to say that all men view the concept as threatening or that all women view it as empowering, but that such a simple word can have a lot of power behind it.

That being the case, to me womanhood is about humble empowerment. Humble because it is what it is, and no sense of braggart is needed to explain it to those who comprehend what it means.

> Because I have yet to meet a woman who loves herself and her body unconditionally **#YesAllWomen**
>
> *@MissAlexisJones*

Womanhood is a camaraderie of understanding, and from that understanding can come sisterhood. As women we are faced with many obstacles that are not easy, and women have faced such obstacles since the beginning of time and thus empathize on a global scale.

However I do not think that womanhood is just about the overcoming of familiar obstacles. More so, it is about the beauty of the gifts of comprehension women can see in themselves and in others who understand.

It is the beauty of strength, motherhood, sisterhood, and in essence, many times, love.

by **Anne**

Role model

by **Elizabeth**

Barrier
breaking it

burning it
bubbling out
skin
mouth
gape
bloody thigh gap.

There are thousands of ways to die inside
infinite ways to be reborn
until the dirt swallows us back
mother
reaching
for father star.

If I had a wish today
it would be a new life,
started like mine
but not erased under the demands
of purgatory
wait your turn
speak politely
under the demands of

marry me
wait for me
hold this
no, it's not your turn yet.

Remember how it started
flash of light
blood everywhere
a cry.

No filth in my words
there's no filth in me but what you
imagine my pounding blood holds
as if your tales could make the curves of me

as if I am not more ancient than your monuments.

by **Anne**

Vulnerable

by **Sabrinna**

Despite being from different hemispheres, towns, cities and populations, we all seem to have been taught such similar things about being women. The feminine role is taught stringently.

It feels like a slight against women that happens in one place has an effect on us all. It matters to us all.

Irrespective of the title, womanhood is its own thing, deviant from *normal* (read *male*) and taught in a most detailed manner no matter where in the world we are.

by **Anne**

STRONG

#YesAllWomen each gender needs the other, in some way. So why can't all members of each gender respect their own and each other?

@ACurrantbun

CHAPTER 10

If you really knew me...

So much of what we show to the world is a false front – the safe mask that we put on so that we'll appear appropriate, friendly, inoffensive, "womanly." It's a part of us, but it's not all of us.

Imagine an M&M – if you tried to predict the taste of the entire candy by what you see on the outside, you would think that it's nothing more than a sugar shell. You would have no idea that inside there is not only chocolate, but perhaps a peanut, an almond, a pretzel. How could you possibly know that from just looking at the candy coating?

> **#YesAllWomen**
> **because people who read my strong writing consistently assume I'm a man. Even when my picture is right next to it.**
>
> *@UVGKassi*

It's true for almost every person in our culture – the outer shell is real, but it doesn't even hint at 99% of what is inside.

In the process of this workshop, the *You Are Not Alone*

writers have cracked their outer shells and allowed themselves to speak their true feelings. Here is one of the very first things they wrote in our time together, talking about pieces of themselves that they don't always show to the world.

by **Sabrinna**

I've come so far.
I've tried so hard.

It isn't easy to be open and trusting after starting life in an unsafe place. It's hard to gauge who is trustworthy when all I have is examples of who isn't.

My "self" fractured into so many parts and I struggled to look whole. The fight back to myself is daily, weekly, year by year.

If you knew me, you wouldn't judge so harshly when I stumble, when my words aren't flowing, clear and concise. When I can't live up to the idealized version you expect.

You would know I wear a mask to protect myself because I was taught I need it to survive.

You would know how hard it is for me to share any skill or talent, because I have been belittled and scorned for the places where I am strong.

Sabrinna

If you knew me, you'd know I can't be everything at once. I can't be confident and inferior. I can't be independent and incapable. I can't be capable and needy.

I've not been invited to feel proud of my skills and talents. I've been told not to 'show-off', not to 'flaunt it', not even to use them lest I appear arrogant or superior. I've been on the end of scathing, nasty words: 'you should,' 'you didn't,' 'you think this,' 'you feel that,' 'I think that you…'

I've not been asked what I think or how I feel. I have been told. I feel invisible. I feel mute.

And I'm tired of toeing a line that has to be strong, capable, secure, independent…

…and simultaneously, only just barely capable, not as good as any man around me.

I have to be confident while being 'put in my place.'

If you knew me, you would know I can't be all those things at the same time. I can't be confident and inferior. I can't be independent and incapable, I can't be capable and needy.

If you knew me, you would know how far I've come.

by **Ashley**

If people really knew me, they would know that I yearn for equality. That I hold everyone – regardless of gender – to the same standard.

When you say, "Not All Men" or "Screw feminism, I'm an equalist," it's once again shifting the focus from the women pushing for equality and placing it on men with a deflated ego.

If people really knew me, they would know that I protest

the dress code because it is sexist and heteronormative, not because I just want to wear cute shorts. They would know that I was told we had a dress code because somebody got raped. They would hold back their disappointed head shakes, and hold back their "slut" accusations. They would know that using those words is the very reason we need feminism.

> # When I was assaulted, I never reported it as I thought no one would believe me because I'm fat. Happens more often than you think. **#YesAllWomen**
>
> *@crixlee*

If people really knew me, they would know I am much more than my blonde hair. They would look past my physical appearance, and realize there is so much more. They would know that I'm one more "make me a sandwich" from bursting.

If people really knew me, they would understand that this so-called "feminist phase" isn't going to blow over.

by **Anne**

I attended a women's college, where I learned to feel that I was equal to anyone, that I could do anything I set out to do, and that gender made no difference.

Then I entered the working world and learned that true equality and partnership are elusive, that men do earn more than women, even in situations where they are less talented and productive than their female colleagues.

I moved into the nonprofit arena, heavily dominated by

women who are pulled by their hearts rather than their wallets.

My own husband has never understood why I want to do the work I do, why I don't strive to grab a corporate job with a hefty salary and generous benefits.

> **#YesAllWomen**
> because hitting, kicking, or throwing "like a girl" is considered the same as weakness.
>
> *@Telescopial*
> *Chloe Beth Wray*

And here is where the greatest show of inequality and non-partnership exists… in my marriage. Certainly we started out in a similar place: a low-paid arts administrator and a poor graduate student. We didn't strive for a lot, wanted to live simply, didn't care about fancy high-paying jobs in fast-paced communities.

But over time, I find a chasm growing. My husband has almost always made more money than me, and he resents having to pay the bulk of the bills. His father worked hard and made a fortune, while his mother stayed at home with the children. And yet somehow he feels that his "partner" needs to contribute an equal amount, financially, to the home.

The subjects of equality and partnership are at the core of my being.

More precisely, inequality and lack of partnership are the cornerstones of my adult life.

by **Leah N.**

If people knew me, they would know that I have a gentle heart. It's soft and it breaks easily, so I keep it hidden beneath sarcasm and education. Inside I have beaten down the artist and raised up the scientist. I don't express emotions easily anymore. I am not sentimental and romantic in mainstream ways, but rather thoughtfulness and kindness speak to me.

I don't keep up with the news because the cynicism and negativity is overwhelming, and it makes me feel hopeless. I am targeted and specific about the social issues and even the people that I care about. I cannot read about starving children and global warming because I get immobilized into inaction.

But sometimes, like with the tragedy in Santa Barbara, I find an opening of hope. The chime of women's voices has come together to speak out about how necessary and real feminism is. And it has been heard around the world.

Hope brings together women from faraway places who need to find those connections, reach out to allies, and move words into action.

#

#YesAllWomen isn't about demonizing men, it's about raising awareness that we need to raise young men to respect women.

@AshNicoleThom

CHAPTER 11

Talking to our younger selves

One theme that showed up frequently in the women's writing was how young they were when they started experiencing verbal and physical harassment and recognizing bias due to their gender. The harassment started around the same time that their bodies began developing. Often, there was no one there to guide them through the wilds. It begged the question: was there anything that someone could have said or done that might have helped to ease the transition into womanhood?

I asked them to imagine talking with themselves at 12 years old and offering the words of advice and comfort to themselves that they wish someone else had given to them at the time.

by **Ashley**

Dear 12-Year-Old Me,

Sometimes we fear that we are just stirring the pot, when

in reality we have been thrown in the pot.

Love,
A Stronger Me

P.S. Continue wearing your retainer. You'll have to go through a second phase of braces.

by **Rachel**

Dear 12-year-old Rachel,

I wish someone had told you that your body is perfect just the way it is.

I wish someone had told you that there's a natural pace at which we're allowed to develop.

I wish someone had sat down with you, held your hand, looked you in the eye and asked you what you were afraid of, what embarrassed you, what you were thinking about.

> #
> **#YesAllWomen** because I'm sitting in Starbucks near a large group of teenage boys and I'm terrified to walk past them to leave.
>
> *@Ciarasaurs*

There was no one there.

But what would they have said? Who in this world is honestly woman enough to say: I understand you feel pressure to perform for boys. I understand you feel pressure to look a certain way. Who could sit me down, hold all of my fears, all of the pressure I felt, all the ideas of where worth comes from?

Perhaps this is the thing that's hard to realize – that sometimes the world does feel ugly. The unjustness of it is real.

What do I, as a woman, really have to say to the 12-year old girl now?

You were loved.
You are loved.
You were always loved.

What do I really want for her?
What does she really want?

For someone to stand next to her, to hold her hand, when I'm in small shorts, when I'm in leopard bras; to say to her, it doesn't have to be this way; to hold her hand and be strong; to say, I love you, you don't have to do that, you don't have to say that.

She is standing there in short shorts.

She's walking with friends at night in the dark.

She wants a kind woman to take her hand, to banish all the kids' laughter and criticism and judgmental thoughts about parents, supervision, being a prude.

To take her hand, standing on the street, and say, "Stop. It doesn't have to be this way. "

by **Mercedes**

Me at 12… I groan at the thought of it.

Okay. But me and talking about my body at that age? What?!

But why would I not want to talk about puberty or sex to my 12-year-old self, when every weekend my conversations with the girls fall along the same lines? Well, that's just the thing, my 12-year-old self was quite clueless about all of this and, frankly, embarrassed.

My mother hadn't learned anything from her mother, and she was 16 when she first started having kids. In many ways she was still growing up herself as she raised the four of us. As the first girl… well, lets just say I didn't get the best "talk."

When I first began my cycle, I kept it a secret. When my body began to change, I did whatever I could to hide it. I learned to be ashamed of my body at a very young age.

> Because girls are taught worldwide that their hymen is the most valuable thing about them. **#YesAllWomen** #purityisajoke #ifonlymenhadhymens
>
> *@love_an_artist*

My mother never talked to me about any of this, and I was horrified when my family found out that I'd gotten my period. I don't think my father meant any harm in joking about it or telling my brothers and their friends about it, but I still remember how angry I was. I still remember running to my room and hating myself. I still remember crying.

I still remember a lot of things about that time.
I remember other women in my family mocking the fact that my breasts weren't fully developed.
I remember being constantly reminded that I was too fat.
I remember my mother staying silent on the subject.
I remember the other girls laughing at me for not shav-

ing my legs.
And I remember grabbing my father's shaving cream and razor to try and do it myself.

That is the theme of it all: I had to learn all these lessons myself.
I had to learn that I am a sexy, bold, and beautiful woman by myself.
I had to learn that my womanhood was NOT something that I should be ashamed of.

The fact that I had a younger sister to look out for further inspired this, as I made certain that many of the obstacles I had faced did not befall her. I made sure she loved every part of herself.

So, what would I have told my 12-year-old self? My 12-year-old sister? Daughter? Niece? Friend? Random woman on the street? I would have told all of them a truth that sadly many women are not privy to: that we are ALL beautiful.

Our bodies are beautiful, the change we undertake is beautiful, and sex on our terms and with a person we love is beautiful.

The shame and competition women face is what corrupts this truth, but this does not have to be the case. In fact,

Our bodies are beautiful, the change we undertake is beautiful, and sex on our terms and with a person we love is beautiful.

Mercedes

many cultures celebrate the "change" and welcome it as what it is – a celebration of becoming a woman, which is a beautiful thing.

> **#YesAllWomen**
> because a man's hormones are an excuse for his behaviour yet mine render me incapable of leadership
>
> *@rosc0e_*

I don't understand why any society would make a woman feel shame. Looking back, I don't think that my parents wished to bring this shame upon their 12-year-old daughter. They probably didn't even consciously know the consequences of their actions. I think it was a lack of awareness, a lack of education about their actions and words.

This is what I think needs to change: We need to inspire strength and pride in our girls, not shame or fear in the face of womanhood.

by **Elizabeth**

When I was 12,
I already knew the thigh
gap, erogenous zones,
weak moans to emulate
porn.

I knew the squeeze
of tight clothes before
the weight of breasts or true unrest.

If someone had told me

my brain and heart
were heavier organs,
that I was only ever meant
to weigh the mass of stars,

I might have known
that all the mysteries of the world
wait for me in the darkest
corners
and have nothing to do with alleys,
scuffed knees.

The grit of mountains
could have bitten my palms
instead of my broken teeth
learning the taste
of flesh between them.

by **Leah N.**

Dear Leah,

I know that this is scary and that you hate change. It will get better, I promise. You don't have to be okay with everything that is happening, but you don't have to be ashamed either.

Just because you get your period doesn't mean that life will change. You don't have to give up swimming or dance. All of this is manageable, and it has happened to women for thousands of years.

There is no rush. You have time to be picky about what boys you want to date. You have time to evaluate the people you want in your life. The most important thing is to choose people who love you, even when you set a boundary. Love and respect cannot exist without each other.

You don't owe anybody anything. Your smile is something that needs to be earned. Your body will change, and your hormones will go crazy. But remember that every choice you make has to be lived with for the rest of your life.

Everyone is scared. They may pretend that they aren't, but this is new for all kids. Wear what makes you happy. Stand up for yourself and for those who can't stand up for themselves.

> # When a man says no in this culture, it's the end of the discussion. When a woman says no, it's the beginning of a negotiation. **#YesAllWomen**
>
> *@Ramen_Hair*

Most of all, don't rush.
You have the rest of your life ahead of you.

by **Crysti**

Dear 12-year-old Crysti,

Hi there, kid!

I wish you could see yourself and how much fun you are having. When you are 39 and someone asks you what your favorite times were, these middle-school years are what you are going to answer.

Enjoy these years. The swim team will be so awesome. You'll even go to the Junior Olympics next year. You'll psych yourself out and just do okay. But that is perfectly fine.

You will remain friends with Lisa for a lifetime. You and Leslie will lose touch and then reconnect as adults and stay lifetime best friends.

But here is what I want you to really, truly know:

Sex is beautiful. You need to be safe. I wish someone would tell you that when you get older and fall in love for the first time, you don't have to be so afraid of going to hell for normal sexual thoughts and feelings.

You can embrace your body as your own. I wish you could somehow block out all of those purity myths that make you become anorexic when you start growing boobs.

Don't quit things you love for a boy. DO NOT quit PATS to keep a guy interested. You and your friends will cross out more "4-ever" names in two-week intervals over the next few years than you can imagine.

Your brains will help you. They will feed your soul. Eventually, they will feed your children. And when you think about their education, you will relive those stories of kite building, beach field trips, soda-pop stock market, learning computers back when disks were huge and floppy and you had to write four lines to draw a box on the screen.

It's okay to wonder what the boys think. They are thinking about potty humor with their buds.

Your mom is human. She loves you and is doing the best she can. Thirty-two is so young. She is not ancient and wise. She loves you with all of her heart. Cut her some slack. Don't judge her by Mrs. Cleaver. She is teaching you more than Mrs. Cleaver ever could have. As a matter of fact, at 39 you will teach a store clerk how to figure depreciation because you studied it with your mom late into the night. Go easy on her.

Call your dad. He actually cares even though he lives far away and acts like once a year is enough dad-ing for him. He has an illness called bipolar, and he will die when you are 25. So just call him. Even if you call him "hey" instead of dad and say "um" on the phone. Even if he never does more than that once-a-year summer thing. He's just a grown kid, and he's trying to figure out how to do life. So "um" if you have nothing to say. But reach out and try.

You are as smart as the not-shy kids. You don't have to be not-shy to be powerful. Don't worry about what everyone thinks of you. Just enjoy your friendships.

These are the best days of your life.

Swim, baby girl, swim.
Love,
Your 39-year-old self

#

#YesAllWomen because I now know that my mum isn't an ultra feminist like society led me to believe, just standing up for herself and her daughters.

@aliceparker0101

A teen's perspective on being a woman

#YesAllWomen have been told they were asking for it.

#YesAllWomen have been told their clothing warrants harassment.

#YesAllWomen have been told they should "act like a lady."

#YesAllWomen have been told they should no longer speak out about their experiences.

#YesAllWomen have been told they are too "pretty" to be anything more than that – just pretty.

#YesAllWomen have been told they should diet.

#YesAllWomen have been told that women with muscles are "gross."

#YesAllWomen are afraid of walking alone at night.

#YesAllWomen should care about these everyday instances of sexism.

#YesAllWomen should care about **#YesAllWomen.**

-- *Ashley*

CHAPTER 12

Acknowledging our experience

According to statistics published by the Rape, Abuse & Incest National Network, there are an average of 237,868 sexual assaults in the United States each year – or, said another way, a woman is sexually assaulted once every two minutes in the United States. Of those, a full 60% are never reported.

But rape and violent assault are not the only ways that women experience violence. There is also verbal harassment on the streets, uninvited groping in bars, and misogynistic treatment in the workplace...to name just a few.

And because it is such a common experience, much of the time we don't even talk about it unless the incident is egregious. It's not that we don't notice it, but when something happens so consistently, talking about it can seem pointless. And in work or home situations, speaking up can often lead to retribution.

The #YesAllWomen conversation on social media in the weeks following the Isla Vista shootings was profound because it started an old conversation in a new way. Hundreds of thousands of voices spoke out at the same time to acknowledge the harassment, bias, and misogyny that are the hallmarks of everyday womanhood.

Standing alone, the Tweets are profound, but there is so much more to the story than can be said in 140 characters. The *You Are Not Alone* writers were able to explore their stories at greater length through the course of this writing workshop. But even this is only the beginning of a long-overdue open conversation about an age-old problem.

by **Leah N.**

It started when I was 11, this blossoming of misogyny.

I felt incredibly free as a child. I was creative and artistic. I danced.

As I grew older, I began to feel pressure to conform to expectations. There were the expectations from my parents.

I remember my father coming to me to have a talk on the porch. His words are still so clear. "Leah, you have to be careful of what you wear. Grown men already follow you around."

I didn't really understand what that meant, or the impact that it would have on my life. I look back to that little girl, still playing with Barbies, climbing trees and playing dress-up games, and wonder how different my life would be if I'd been a boy.

My dad said that if I wanted to work at a fast food restaurant, he would support that choice, but in the same conversation told me he was jealous of my potential. I heard sharp, cutting words from him like, "You've never worked for anything in your life. Everything just falls into your lap, and you don't deserve it."

From my mother I got messages about my body and how it didn't meet her expectations. I remember being 7 years old and being told that I was too old to have "baby fat" lingering. She told me at 12 to stop eating so much because even my fingers were fat.

I have failed both of my parents by not living up to their expectations.

I watched the after-school specials and was convinced that I would be raped to death.

> Because a woman in my town was repeatedly drugged and raped by her husband and the judge told her to forgive him. **#YesAllWomen**
>
> *@AllisonLCarter*

I remember being followed home.

Not being able to get into my own home without being touched by strange men.

Men who tell you to smile, as though you are only there to look pretty.

Women who police clothing and repeat victim blaming, enforcing sexist cultural norms.

Both my insides and out were put on display, dissected, diagnosed and told to fit into boxes. Boxes I didn't understand or like.

by **Ashley**

My talk of equality had scared him.

"Feminazi!" he screamed. In defense of his privilege, to comfort his ego.

He would later argue for the use of the word. He said, "These words aren't offensive to me."

He said, "Words only hold the power you give them."

Hopeless, I cried. No matter what, no matter how sound my argument was, my adversary would attack me with ad-hominem fallacies, and my voice would be reduced to "Feminazi."

by Crysti

Women seem to hate each other.

I just watched a movie with Sarah Jessica Parker where working moms judge kindergarten room moms and vice versa. It seemed so real to me. Some were exaggerations, but it rang very true.

> #
> A man on the street told me I needed to cover up cause I was making him think impure thoughts. I was wearing a t-shirt and jeans. **#YesAllWomen**
>
> *@lynnbixenspan*

I think women hating women is real. But men play into it readily.

At my old law firm, they picked pretty girls to be summer associates. One summer they hired two summer associates who were engaged, and my boss said, "Well, that missed the whole point."

It makes me sad that sexual harassment is so rampant. And it's never consensual.

by **Elizabeth**

Life drifted slowly back
to me,
taste of
cotton
syrup
mouth
from the previous night's fruity
concoction.

If everyone knew what
you knew...

I said "hold still."
He said "it's not enough."

Layer the trigger.

Lip-smack against my ear.

Tell me, trigger,
tell me what you saw so
I know what happened to me that
night,

Know if I was fighting
hard enough for it to mean "no,"
if I wore something that "had it coming."

by **Leah C.**

I was 12 and away from home for the first time – three whole weeks on a college campus for a summer program. But I wasn't accustomed to being so far from home for so long, and I was terribly homesick.

My dad's idea: a young friend and colleague of his was going to be in Boston. Why not have Ryan come over and take me out for dinner? It would give me a taste of home while I was away.

Ryan was 26, a writer, someone who had been around our home a lot. But he was Dad's friend, not mine. As a 12-year-old girl, I was too shy to even speak to a guy of that age.

And he didn't show up alone. No, Ryan brought along one of his buddies I'd never met. Two 20-somethings with a 12 year old girl. Nothing good could come of this. And worse, they were driving a two-seater car. Yep, nowhere for the young girl to sit except on one of their laps or on the hump between them.

We went to get pizza. I don't remember much about it except that it seemed extremely awkward.

Finally…finally…finally! It was time for them to drive me back to the dorm. But instead of going straight there, they took a detour. Up into the woods. Into an area that I had never seen before. An area where there were no other lights, no other people, no safety.

I asked them to take me back to the dorm and they said, "In a little bit."

I was certain that I was about to be assaulted and raped. Perhaps even killed. My 12-year-old brain was imagining every worst-case-scenario, but too paralyzed to even speak. There was nothing to do but sit between them and wait.

> **#YesAllWomen**
> because men call you a slut for sleeping with them, and because men call you a slut when you don't sleep with them
>
> *@CarlitaMcLucas*

Nothing did happen that night. I have no recollection of why they took me up into the woods – perhaps to have a cigarette? That's the only thing I can even muster as a possible explanation, but really I have no idea. After a while, they returned me to my dorm, none the worse for wear.

Except that I was. I was TERRIBLY the worse for wear. I had just lived through a ripping apart of my young soul. A vital piece of myself was shorn away that night – whatever trust, safety, control over my own body I might have felt before that night was now gone.

Once back in the dorm, I went to my RA and had a complete nervous breakdown. She called my parents, unsure of what to do. I don't remember anything after that. It's amazing how much the mind can block out.

But I am left with this lingering question: What father sends his 12-year-old daughter out with a 26-year-old man in a strange place with no protections in place?

And perhaps all of that could have been forgiven. Perhaps it's fair to say that my dad couldn't have foreseen the particular circumstances. Perhaps it's fair to think that he really just wanted to do something nice for me when he knew that I was so homesick. Perhaps he really was just trying to be a good and loving father.

But this is the part that I still struggle with all these years later: when I got home from camp, my dad said, "He's a good guy. You have an overactive imagination."

I desperately needed my dad to understand how scared I was. This was no longer about whether Ryan was a good guy or not. This was about how petrified I had been and the loss of innocence I had experienced. But my dad could only say, "He's a good guy."

He chose to protect his friend rather than protecting his little girl.

He continued inviting Ryan over to our house. And every time I saw him, I lost another little piece of my soul.

> #
>
> Because even as I'm reading **#YesAllWomen** my gut reaction is to minimize, justify, and assume at least part of the blame for my own abuse.
>
> *@emilypostpunk*

by **Crysti**

Dear Person on the Internet,

It sounds like you think it is wrong to even discuss ways in which women protect themselves from attack. That we should leave it to "karma" to take care of the situation.

I would love to think that karma was enough to get the bad guys. But women who are real victims don't want to be part of some great cosmic experiment for karma to prove itself.

Yes, let's talk about making the world a nicer and better place. But women are afraid to walk down the street in some places – really almost all places – alone after dark.

There is a real need to talk about that, to bring attention to how it is for women vs. men who take walking alone after dark for granted.

If I misunderstood your criticism, please help me understand. How is asking the question not moving the dialogue forward?

by Elizabeth

I would much rather be able
to name the nebulas for you
than spot what a guy would like
from the way he hunches, walks,
where his eyes linger or when they
dart away, but my education was
different from yours. If only
I could say it was different
from most girls.

When I was in middle school,
I was already used to hands
wandering over me, the feeling
of chills up and around me,
teaching me my body was only
borrowed, not my own unless
no one had use of it.

Elizabeth

I would much rather be able to name the nebulas for you than spot what a guy would like from the way he hunches, walks....

CHAPTER 13

Being heard

Some of what we face as women stems from our culture teaching us to "not worry our pretty little heads." We learn not to speak up and let our voices be heard. Certainly great strides have been made in recent decades, but there's a long way to go. Our mothers' and grandmothers' voices still linger in our heads as instructions for how to be acceptable as a woman.

> # Because I constantly assume I'll be called stupid for being scared of my emotional abuser. #YesAllWomen
>
> *@sarcasticvoice*

I invited the women to write a letter to someone – or tell a story about someone – who hadn't listened to them. It gave them an opportunity to finally say the words that they have been wanting the other person to hear.

Research shows that when we hold on to upsetting experiences without giving them expression, our thoughts about those experiences grow darker and more twisted.[5] While the

[5] Pennebaker JW. *Opening Up: The Healing Power of Emotional Expression*. New York, NY: Guilford Publications; 1997.

addressee of the women's letters may never read or hear their words, simply giving expression to them brings healing by getting the words out of their heads.

by **Anne**

When I was in my twenties, I received a notice from the DMV saying that my license would be suspended because I had committed a traffic violation and did not show up in court. I was astounded, because this had not actually happened. I was nowhere near the place this allegedly occurred on the date noted.

I went to the state DMV to plead my case. The man behind the counter kept insisting I had committed a violation. I kept trying to explain that it was not me, I had not been in that place or done that thing.

I was in tears and angry, and I started to swear because I couldn't make him understand me. That only made him angry, and he told me I would be in even greater trouble because of it.

Finally he figured out that there was another woman in the state with my name, that the violation was hers. I was free to go.

But I felt wounded. I was incredibly hurt because I knew I was innocent but was not believed or heard. I felt helpless.

Another time, soon after the birth of my son. My husband was about to leave for a teaching assignment in Europe. My son and I were to follow two months later.

I was making iced tea and was distracted. I poured nearly boiling water into a glass pitcher that was not Pyrex. It shattered and hot water splashed on my ankle, seriously burning me. I was on crutches for weeks and had to go on an IV antibiotic for infection.

Rather than expressing his concern for my wellbeing, my husband lashed out at me, telling me how stupid I'd been and suggesting I'd done it on purpose because I didn't want to move abroad.

> **#YesAllWomen**
> Because homophobia is the fear that another man will treat you the way you treat women.
>
> *@Shanny_Dawe*
> *Shannon Dawe*

While I was indeed sorry to leave a new job I really liked, I had no qualms about moving overseas – in fact, I looked forward to a new adventure. I certainly hadn't planned an accident to get out of it.

Though I tried to explain, he couldn't hear me.

As it turned out, an old girlfriend of his had once purposely broken her leg to avoid doing something, and he was so stressed out about moving overseas and teaching in a foreign country that he transferred his anxiety to me.

I felt hurt, abandoned, helpless. I felt grief that the partner I knew seemed to have disappeared. It took years of counseling to heal that rift.

by **Elizabeth**

Dear
  Sir
    Madam

mistress,
    fellow,
person on the bus who said
"she had it coming."

  Count the seconds of your
life,
   time spent buying
coffee
  laughing with
friends

dancing with mother.
   Tell me it would be enough
ended with tasting fist
and your own blood.

  This sickness
      thickness
ego-blatant.
   Trivialize my smiles
for how much you
can see of my thighs.

  Down-damned firebrand.
 Home-wrecking
    howling
    heathen.

I've laid the ground work
for my misery, you said.

Grand-stand morality
      on my grave.

by **Leah N.**

Dear R,

When we met, I didn't have much experience of the world, much less of men. I didn't know how deep those waters were and how full of sharks.

Do you remember the things that you did to me? I know you felt my fear, because I could see it in your face. I remember that you used to cry sometimes, as if I was the one who hurt you.

What was it about me that caught your eye? Was it the way that I smiled? Was it the mischievous look in my eye? Was it simply my innocence? I never thought to ask you, and now I never will.

I should have trusted myself when I broke up with you the first time. And the second. And every time after that. But it took me three years to leave.

Do you know how many times you transgressed? Do you know how many times you took what you wanted, without thinking or caring? I don't.

I'll forgive you all the guilt. But that doesn't get us very far,

I look at pictures of your daughter and I hope that her high school sweetheart is completely unlike you. I hope that you don't learn about men like you through her.

Leah

now, does it?

You took something from me. Bigger than the physical. You stole my voice. I learned to compress all of my emotions and my needs inside myself. Compact it into a small box. It's been locked so long that the key is rusty and I don't know how to open it anymore.

> So when you argue semantics, it feels like what you're saying is that our experiences matter less than your interpretation. **#YesAllWomen**
>
> *@vqnerdballs*

I have tried to forgive you. I don't know if I can. I don't know if I want to.

I regret you. And I am sorry for you. I wonder if you still take and take until the world around you is empty. But don't get too full of yourself, because I don't think about you so often.

I'm better off without you. I can see the world with kindness.

Though I do still keep my distance, wondering what is behind the façade of every person I meet. I am cautious in my relationships. You taught me that trust is earned, and slowly. My heart is harder than it was.

I'm not the same anymore. Mostly, I'm better. Stronger and more sympathetic. More thoughtful. I have better boundaries. I'm getting my voice back. Men like you have no place in my life.

I look at pictures of your daughter on Facebook, and I wonder. I hope that no man like you comes into her life.

I hope that her high school sweetheart is someone completely unlike you. I hope he is someone with gentle hands and kind words. Someone who desires her mind and strives to understand all that is in her heart. She deserves laughter and light and love. Respect and honesty. But I don't know who will teach her that those are the things she should expect from her boyfriend.

It makes me so sad when I see her picture.

Mostly, I hope that you don't learn about men like you through your daughter.

You probably thought my letter was about you? But really, it's about me.

by **Sabrinna**

Dear John,

I know, to this day, you have no idea why I broke up with you and I wonder if you'll ever understand that a relationship is a partnership, not a battleground of constant accusation and put-downs.

For years you tried to get me back, but it will never happen because I have not forgotten. I couldn't trust you even with the most minor detail about myself. The words, "You think you're better than everyone else," are not an appropriate response to hearing what I care about. "I don't believe you" is not an appropriate response when I told you how I felt.

Relationships are about trust. There is nothing to trust when words are met with combative hostility.

I pretend to be your friend now. I only do it for the benefit of our mutual friends. I pretend, when really, I want nothing to do with you. I do it only to keep the peace. Don't email me. Don't ask me to meet you somewhere. It was "no." It is "no." The answer has been NO the whole time.

> # I want a world where every sexist guy trolling meets two or more guys who say "Dude, stop it, you're being an asshole." **#YesAllWomen**
>
> *@ThinkHaddad*

Your constant badgering is inappropriate. For goodness sake, take a hint. Notice how you don't have my address, my phone number, my social media ID. Notice how I only see you by chance at gatherings. Notice how I never tell you anything about myself and keep the conversation brief and superficial.

Notice, when I told you it was over, I never once faltered. When I said I didn't want to hang out one-to-one, I stuck to my word. If years of badgering hasn't worked, why on earth would you think, 'just one more', will? It won't.

Please leave me alone.

by **Elizabeth**

Trust
   Fragile cracks, fine as hairs
across my face,
  tears over lips like salt licks. I
looked up to you with heart in
eyes, ready to be broken.

  If I could say one thing to

you it would be, "Don't worry. I
took my world back. It wasn't
all about you and the tar inside
us, after all."

by **Leah C.**

Dear man who messaged me on the internet dating site,

Your profile concludes, "If I email you, please email me back. I took the time to write to you, the least you can do is send a message in response."

I wish that I could honor your request. I really do. It would be the kind thing to do. But I can't, and I want to explain to you why.

Early in my internet dating days, I believed that I needed to respond to every message I received. I wanted to be polite.

A man contacted me saying I had a cute smile and it was too bad that we would probably never meet. I was puzzled – why contact a potential date and tell them up front that you'll probably never meet? Between his profile and his strange message, it was clear that he wasn't my cup of tea. But other than a mismatch in personalities and communication styles, there was nothing about his profile that pinged my internal safety alarms.

I struggled over how to respond to his peculiar message and landed on something extremely noncommittal like, "Thank you for your message. I hope you have a nice day."

A couple weeks later, I was at the ATM at my local bank branch when a man came running over to my car. He got between my car and the machine and stuck his head through my car window.

"You're the girl from Match.com, aren't you!? You're the one who told me to have a nice day!!! What does that mean?? What's the problem? Am I not your type??"

> # Unfortunately we all have a lot of these stories. If you're tired of hearing them, imagine how tired we are of living them. **#YesAllWomen**
>
> *@annedeacetis*

I was frozen. I couldn't stay and I couldn't go. Perhaps the smart thing would have been to drive off, but another fear crept up – what if his head or neck got injured as I drove off and then he sued me? Crazier things have happened. Plus, my card was still in the ATM and damned if I was going to leave identifying information for him to retrieve as soon as I was gone.

I tried to laugh it off, as if he must certainly be joking.

***

During the summer months I enjoy watching the CBS reality show Big Brother. It's a fluffy diversion that is guaranteed to be unpredictable.

Until this year, I was strictly a primetime TV watcher. But in the summer of 2014, I was intrigued by the "Zankie" showmance that flirted with the possibility of a young man exploring new aspects of his sexuality and a gay relationship developing in the house. I started paying closer attention to social media and even dipped my toes into the live feeds.

What I discovered below the surface chilled me.

Upon entering the house, houseguest Caleb quickly became obsessed with fellow houseguest Amber. He told her he liked her and he knew she liked him back. She said, "Not really." He told her that they were destined to get married. She politely backed away. She said she wanted to be friends.

> Because men don't text each other that they got home safe. #YesAllWomen
>
> @wheresaddie

They were locked in the same house for the summer, so there were limited places she could run. She made it clear that she wasn't interested, but Caleb didn't let up. He pushed and pushed. When her position in the game was in danger, he offered to sacrifice himself to save her. She told him not to. He did it anyway and then acted as though she owed him for his great act of honor. He frequently referred to her as "My queen" and became aggressive with other guys who spent time with her.

If there weren't cameras on them 24/7, I would have been legitimately concerned for this girl's safety. This is Stalker 101 behavior.

As disturbing as the situation on TV was, the commentary in social media was even more so. Amber was repeatedly slut-shamed on social media.[6] She was accused of being too nice to him and giving him hope.

---

[6] Slut-shaming is the act of judging or degrading a woman for being "too sexual." It can be based on the actions, words, clothing or any other quality of a woman. In some cases, women are slut-shamed for the assumption of their sexual exploits, even when their actions show the contrary.

One commenter says, "It's Amber's fault. If she just liked him back, it would seem sweet instead of creepy."

It's not enough that she clearly said "No" every time he made an advance. According to the mores of our internet culture, she was supposed to cut him off at the knees. Never mind that if she did that, the very same people would have called her even worse names and sympathy would have gone to Caleb. As it was, her chances at a half million dollars were eliminated when Caleb turned against her for being ungrateful.

And all of this through no fault of hers. It's simply because she is the target of a man's affections.

Perhaps the most disturbing thing I've seen is this seemingly silly poll on the Entertainment Weekly website:

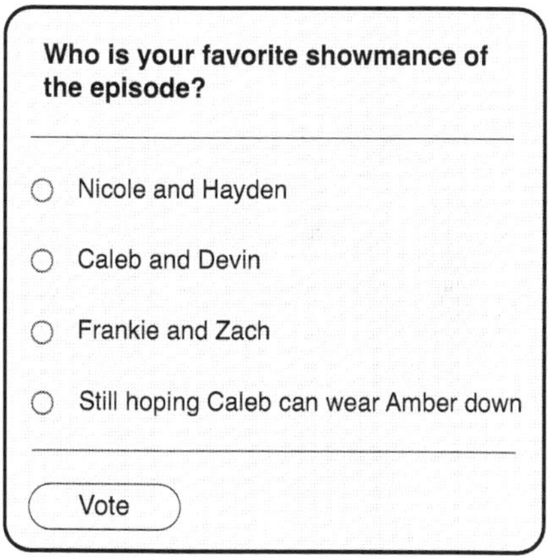

Who is your favorite showmance of the episode?

- Nicole and Hayden
- Caleb and Devin
- Frankie and Zach
- Still hoping Caleb can wear Amber down

Vote

Even a major entertainment news outlet is promoting the idea that if Caleb just works hard enough, he can overwhelm Amber's sense of self and take what he wants.

What is Amber supposed to do? She's damned if she does and damned if she doesn't.

This summer Amber is the placeholder for every one of us who has felt that our position in work/school/ life/etc. would be threatened if we rejected a guy we weren't interested in.

Sadly, too many women have a Caleb story.

***

So, my dear internet suitor, this is why I cannot honor your request with a polite "No, thank you." You may not be anything like the man at the ATM. You are probably nothing like Caleb. But there's no way for me to know in advance. Unfortunately, it is yet another case of the behavior of your brothers creating waves which catch you in the riptide.

I am truly sorry. I feel the hurt behind your words. I know that you must have been rejected and/or ignored a lot of times to feel the need to make that request on your profile. So I apologize on behalf of myself and all of my sisters for the poor treatment you have received at our hands.

> **#YesAllWomen**
> because "no" doesn't mean no until another male steps in and tells him no.
>
> *@vintagxe*

But while silence may seem rude, it is infinitely preferable to the alternative. You are probably not a predator, but I'd rather be safe than sorry.

Thanks for your interest,
Leah

by **Mercedes**

I have learned that just because someone hears you does not necessarily mean that they will listen. I have experienced this all too often. I feel betrayed and ignored when it happens, especially in my family. I present what I assume is a logical answer, only to be ignored or given false reassurances that I have been heard.

Even so, I have learned a lot through these conversations, and it's helpful as I move forward in the field of psychology.

You cannot change people.

People can only change themselves.

When someone is ready for advice, when someone is ready for change, then change will come.

Listening and communicating are precious gifts, and as women we are blessed to be quite ample in this ability. I've learned that gentle encouragements and empathy work best when listening to others. Hopefully, when someone gets to the point where they do desire real change, they will recall your words and remember your empathy. So, make others feel acknowledged, by genuinely empathizing and listening to what they are saying in their times of need.

> # Because when I told a boy off for telling a rape joke in class, I was told to be quiet and to stop overreacting. **#YesAllWomen**
>
> *@hannnah_rose18*

Something that my Tia[7] has told me and that I have always taken to heart is: "Say what you mean, and mean what you say."

Don't be scared to speak your piece, and from the heart. And when you are still not heard or acknowledged in your

[7] "Tia" is the Spanish word for "aunt."

own time of need, find better friends who recognize and love you.

There is no shame in sharing yourself with people you trust. I have found strength and acceptance in my friends, in my sisters. I stand here stronger today because of the bonds I have made with them, the stories we have all shared, and the advice we give and receive.

Value your words, and value who you share them with.

Empathize with all, in the hopes that the kindness will be returned.

Most importantly, believe that *people are doing the best they can.*

> I got more attention for losing weight than earning my master's degree, running a half marathon, or helping build a nonprofit. **#YesAllWomen**
>
> *@HeatherLose*

CHAPTER 14

Questioning "control"

It's a hot-button issue that I address in every workshop I do, and it's always fertile territory: *control.*

When I offered the word to the group, it immediately elicited a groan.

The word brings up mixed emotions for many people because it has so many connotations:
"I don't want to be controlled by someone else."
"I want to be in control of my own life."
"I'm trying to let go of my need to control."

by **Leah N.**

I never felt in control of my life as a child. I wasn't allowed to make many decisions on my own.

Some of that was personality – I have always been a private person.

My mother, to be fair, was simply taking advantage of teaching opportunities, like editing my letters to my childhood pen-pal. She thought she was improving my grammar, spelling and writing skills. I felt like I wasn't free to express myself without being watched.

As I grew older, the control developed into more sinister things. In my relationships, it always felt like someone was winning, and it didn't usually feel like that person was me. Like boyfriends who saw that I was in control of myself and wanted to tame and control me.

I've always had a wild imagination and spirit. Sticking to the rules of anything has always felt restrictive and constricting. It made me feel out of control.

> #
>
> **#YesAllWomen**
> because among my college daughter's school supplies, we felt compelled to buy pepper spray, but not for my nephew.
>
> *@EvaLee71*

I want to feel confident in my authority and autonomy, but I don't yet.

by **Sabrinna**

To me, control is subtle and covert.

Control is facial expressions, gestures, common assumptions, implied meaning, context and subtext.

It's really easy to point to "do this," "don't do that or else..." But without the subtle and covert systemic sexism, the overt words would have little power, standing out as unusual, unjust, abnormal, and obviously wrong.

For example, imagine an unexpected pregnancy. It's so

normal to blame the woman:

Did she do it on purpose to trap the man?
Is it even his?
Was she completely monogamous?

Meanwhile, we don't challenge a man when he accuses, 'You ruined my life,' as though he were not 50% responsible. We judge young mothers as irresponsible, but a young guy is a "fantastic dad" if he just shows up.

Control is billions of assumptions that inform every moment of our lives.

by **Crysti**

I am a control freak. I tend to pick women friends who are also control freaks. Which makes for interesting road trips! I surrender control of the steering wheel, but typically not the decisions like where we are going to stay.

> **#YesAllWomen**
> because I got cursed at and then followed for half a block today after turning down a guy's unwanted advances #nomeansno
>
> *@klabovitz*

Control gets in the way of my relationship with my in-laws. I won't live near them because it is a battle every time we visit – where and when are we going to do things, when are we going to leave, etc. Then we get back late on Sundays when I have work or the boys have school the next day because of the "long goodbye." That means I have good reasons to be a control freak, right?!?

With my kids, I am pretty laissez-faire and start with trust until I catch them lying or getting into trouble. But I start with trust. The parental control thing isn't all that strong.

I definitely am the one that controls the money in our house, which leads to my husband stashing cash. And then I get mad at him for not knowing what the bills are. But I don't really trust anyone else to feed my kids. Not even my husband.

by **Grace**

Control is something that I am very conscious of and working to let go of in all instances: when I feel the need or desire to control, or when I feel someone is attempting to control me.

It stems from fear. Fear of being hurt or trying not to hurt someone else.

Changing this pattern that started before I was born has been challenging. But when I am successful and operating from love and trust, I am much happier and at peace.

I am a woman who enjoys being free above all else. As much as I love children and imagine a life with a partner, it certainly has not been easy to give up my desire to do what I wish, when I wish, how I wish.

by **Elizabeth**

"While you're living in this house, you'll shave your legs," my stepdad said.

I'm grateful to him.

I didn't shave again until I was 18 years old, my first
silent but bold
resounding
NO.

by **Mercedes**

Control is a double-edged sword. It acts both as a form of comfort, while at times it inspires rebellion.

In a positive light, personal control allows for regulation over my own thoughts and emotions, and the way that I choose to express them. It is a control on my inhibitions. It is even a control on my heart and who I choose to love and leave. This side of control is empowering.

The other side of control, the side that inspires my rebellion, comes from everything else. It shows up when anyone else tries to place restrictions or controls on me. I take steps to ensure that it does not happen. I will allow no one to put controls on me that I do not wish to carry.

> #
> **#YesAllWomen**
> because the best way to insult a guy is by calling him a girl
>
> *@BayCamBam*

I value my independence and wisdom. It is from this place that I create my own sense of control.

Relationships are about compromise on both sides, not domination or control.

by **Grace**

Fear has not served me.

I vow to no longer let it control my thoughts, feelings and life.
Afraid of hurting others' feelings, of getting my feelings hurt.
Of people's disapproval, of being stupid.
You name it, I was applying that to the equation.
So sad, but I am finally catching it.
I am looking at it and dismissing it as something that is made up.
It is a separate entity from me.

by **Rachel**

Control is what I don't have right now.
Control is when I try to fix my life over and over again, and nothing works.
Control is when I think that by thinking something, it will happen.

Control is different from listening to my body. My body feels, senses, and can't predict its environment.

Like yesterday, at an art store where I picked up a shabby notebook and used marker and asked for a discount even though I was afraid.

Afterward, as I got in my car in the sunshine, I had the courage to go back, knock on the closed sliding glass door, and return the

Rachel

My power can sometimes be in following and listening, rather than leading and controlling.

plastic bag I wouldn't use. The manager's face registered surprise when he understood why I had returned.

He smiled.
I smiled.
My body felt listened to, alive.

My power can sometimes be in following and listening, rather than leading and controlling.

It's the little things, listening, following our instincts, however small, that lie on the other side of control.

by **Mercedes**

The word "control" reminds me of a saying: "If you find that you can't control your woman, you've found a good one."

by **Elizabeth**

I first experienced discrimination when I was seven years old. My friend took his shirt off in a hot car in the desert of Arizona. My dad shouted at me when I tried to do the same.

Starting at age eight, men were already taking pictures of me without my permission. Schoolboys pressured me into letting them touch me… and sometimes did so without asking.

Men exposed themselves to me, asked me if I wanted to touch them, tried to convince me to stop by their homes on my way home from school.

Music videos portrayed women as bodies moving to whatever tune the man directing commanded.

As I grew into a teenager, I learned that though I was expected to be sexually pleasing or appealing, I was the last person who got to decide what I wore, how I acted or spoke, and how I could express my growing sexuality.

I raided my parent's porn collection. I read magazines and erotic novels about the best way to give someone pleasure. None of them mentioned the best ways to satisfy women or to be satisfied as a woman.

Sex ed covered the mechanics of sexual activity, but never bothered to mention consent.

At 14, I started homeschooling and hooked in to the internet to an even greater degree. I had all manner of images available instantly at my fingertips. A pornography addiction ensued, and soon nothing would satisfy me but videos and images that got harder, rougher, harsher.

> **#YesAllWomen**
> because when a girl got raped by star athletes, the media talked about their ruined future, not how they ruined her life
>
> *@juliaisslamow*

Despite sexual pressure from every direction, I didn't have a complete sexual relationship until I was 18. A series of short relationships ensued, marked by infidelity masquerading as polyamory or "friendships with benefits." I became a model that same year.

As I entered my 20s, I went from glamour modeling to fetish

modeling. Though I never did full pornography, for years I listened to men tell me how to pose, when and how to grunt, how to walk, what to wear, what made me most attractive, what men wanted wanted wanted from me to satisfy themselves.

After a brief stint at a strip club in Atlanta, I headed to New York City to train as a professional dominatrix at the world-famous dungeon, Pandora's Box.

I returned to Atlanta vicious and ready to conquer. My clients kneeled and kissed my feet, worshipping me and showering me with gifts for the pain I inflicted on them. I learned an important lesson: my submissives were willing participants who trusted me to respect their wishes and never go too far. It was a relationship built on consent. That trust helped break my heart back open. Some of those submissives became long-term friends.

I'm now retired from professional BDSM. I'm in a three-year relationship, the healthiest I've ever experienced. We are equal parties, and we have an open negotiation about our desires.

Sex – even fantasy sex that involves BDSM play – must be consensual. That's something that sex ed never bothered to teach. It's something that the media – in its countless representations of sex, sexuality, and sexual relations – never bothered to teach either.

In sharing my experiences, I hope to move society toward respecting young girls and boys as individuals, rather than training them to be porn stars and perpetrators. I hope we are moving toward a world that builds children into people, instead of commodities and users.

CHAPTER 15

81 ways we avoid harassment and assault

As I was planning this workshop, I was inspired by the story of a university professor who divided his chalkboard in half. He asked the women in the class to call out the things they did to avoid harassment and assault on a daily basis. He quickly filled one half of the chalkboard. He then asked the men in the class to call out the things that they did to avoid harassment and assault. He was met with stunned silence as the students realized that the men didn't have a single answer... because they never think about it.

I asked the *You Are Not Alone* writers the same question. Our group of 10 women brainstormed this list in only 7 minutes.[8]

1. When a guy hits on me, I tell him I've got a boyfriend even when I don't because many guys don't accept "no" as an answer.

[8] A discussion of street harassment against women is often dismissed with the logic, "But men are harassed too." It is certainly true that men experience harassment, and this list and this book are not meant to minimize that fact in any way. A recent national study of harassment in a variety of categories (including unwelcome touching, sexual language, flashing, following, sexual assault, and more) shows that women are on the receiving

2. Use the buddy system when we go out with friends.

3. When going somewhere like the club, go with enough women to maintain a presence.

4. Never smile or say hi when I'm alone.

5. Dance in a group.

6. Make sure my dance moves are not too provocative.

7. Buy my own drinks.

8. Don't get drunk.

9. Pretend I don't speak English.

10. Use a fake name.

11. Have a fake number memorized.

12. Pretend my friends and I are lesbians.

13. Know where to get water in any area.

14. Pull my friends away from someone on the dance floor who creeps up from behind.

15. Make sure I am in eye contact with my girls at all times.

16. Only go out with friends who will take care of me – when I was drunk once, my friend whispered to a man that I was pregnant so he would leave me alone.

> **#YesAllWomen**
> because EVERY time I go out drinking I get my arse slapped/ grabbed then looked at like I'm in the wrong when I challenge them
>
> *@GabbiRoslinxo*

---

end of this behavior 3 to 5 times more often than men. The only exception is homophobic slurs, which men receive 3 times more often than women. A note on the study shows that of the harassment reported by men, a higher percentage of LGBT-identified men were affected than straight men. Read more about this study at http://www.stopstreetharassment.org/our-work/nationalstudy.

17. Control my impulse to dance if there's good music on the PA system in a grocery store because it might be seen as provocative.

18. Don't wear t-shirts that have any words or images that could be interpreted as provocative.

19. Walk the route that has the best lighting and the most amount of open places such as corner stores, clubs, bars, hotels, etc.

20. Get to know the security at local bars and clubs on the routes I walk home – offer them a cigarette and ask how their night is; remember their names, if they have a family, what nights they usually work; make sure they know my name.

21. Use iPhone maps so I know always where I am and how to get home.

22. Never appear lost when I'm walking by myself – go into a store before I pull out my phone to look up directions.

23. Break a banana into pieces before eating it in public.

24. Stay on the phone with someone when walking alone after dark.

25. Don't talk on the phone when I'm alone at night because I don't want to be distracted from small noises and warnings.

26. Pretend I'm on the phone.

> **#YesAllWomen**
> because after replying "Hi" to a strange man's greeting I had to deal with him trying to guess the color of my nipples. ... and I immediately thought "my fault" for replying.
>
> *@angie_pants*

27. Walk briskly and look straight ahead.

28. Ride my bike at top speed down the streets.

29. Avoid certain blocks and alleys.

30. Avoid walking *anywhere* alone, especially after dark.

31. Don't go running at night.

> **#** Because a smile back can get you followed, but no response can get you killed. And neither one guarantees the harassment ends. **#yesallwomen**
>
> *@amanda_ruggeri*

32. Don't go to the beach at night.

33. Carry my keys between my fingers so I can use them as a weapon.

34. Regularly alter my route home whether I'm walking, riding my bike, or driving my car.

35. Walk with my dog, even when he's too sleepy.

36. Avoid wooded areas unless I have my dog with me.

37. Switch to the other side of the street if I see someone coming.

38. Carry an asp and a bayonet for safety.

39. Get a male to escort me to my car after hours.

40. Carry mace on my keychain.

41. Avoid making eye contact or smiling at strange men so they don't think I am flirting.

42. Constantly look behind me.

43. Look down when I pass construction sites or groups of young men hanging out on street corners.

44. Assess people before I pass them to decide whether I feel danger or not.

45. Text friends when I get home to confirm that I'm safe.

46. Always leave lights on at home.

47. Don't answer a knock on the door if I see a strange man on the porch.

48. Double bolt the door when I'm home.

49. Don't pick up hitch-hikers.

50. Don't stop to help people stranded by the side of the road.

> **#** I'm not a tease for letting you buy me a drink and not going home with you. You offered me a drink, not your dick on a plate. **#YesAllWomen**
>
> *@JeskaWillow*

51. Keep my "shit kicker" bat by the door.

52. Worry about whether I should let the delivery man see where I live.

53. Word my outgoing voicemail message so it doesn't sound like I live alone.

54. Don't enter my hotel room door if there's a man in the hall.

55. Don't wear a lot of makeup or revealing clothing.

56. Wear covered up clothes, even in the summer heat.

57. Avoid my manager at work – postpone meetings, meet in a shared space when I do have to see him.

58. Put myself down before a man has a chance, effectively taking his ammunition away from him.

59. Meet male friends and acquaintances out – never have them to my house, unlike female acquaintances.

60. Don't go to a stranger's home.

61. End conversations, even though it can come off as distant or

bitchy.

62. Go places with my tall boyfriend in tow because I feel safer.

63. Use nervous laughter as if an inappropriate comment were a joke, to imply "no way could that be said seriously."

64. If I'm in an elevator alone and a man gets in, I get out.

65. Don't go into an empty elevator or stairwell with a man.

66. Don't accept rides with men.

67. Avoid big city activities after dark.

68. Know where exits and dark places are in parking garages.

69. Don't park near vans.

70. Always park under a street light at night.

71. Carry a fake wallet that I can throw on the ground to distract someone while I run away.

72. Be ready to throw my keys far away from me when leaving the mall so I can distract an attacker while I run away.

> #
> **Because I go through Muay Thai moves in my head while trying to remember where the main artery in the neck is when I walk home #YesAllWomen**
>
> *@Tryphena93*

73. Don't sit in my car for a long time before cranking up and going.

74. Always check the back seat of my car to make sure it's empty before getting in.

75. Walk in the middle of the street.

76. Have a taxi on speed dial.

77. Don't open my car window for a cop who has pulled me over

until seeing their badge.

78. Go to the bathroom in groups.

79. Make up scenarios in my head so I know how I would react.

80. Go places with little kids – it makes me feel safer because I'm seen more as a mom and less as a woman.

81. Imagine that I have two angels, big strong men, visible to others, walking next to me when I'm alone.

> #
>
> I just asked my wife if she worries for her safety when she's alone. She said yes. We've been married 15 years; I never knew. **#YesAllWomen**
>
> *@willsansbury*

CHAPTER 16

Admitting that we're not without fault

It's easy enough to look at our lives and see the injustices that we've experienced. It takes much more courage to look at our lives and see the injustices that we've done to others. And yet it's a vital part of our individual and collective healing and growth.

As long as we see ourselves as victims of a social construct, we are powerless to change it because we will never be able to change anyone else's behavior. But when we see how we participate in that social construct – how we have perpetuated it by our own behavior – we suddenly become much more powerful. When we recognize the ways we participate in the dysfunction, we are able to change our behavior. And every individual who changes his or her behavior contributes to the healing of the entire system.

As Maya Angelou famously said, "When you know better, you do better."

The *You Are Not Alone* writers have shown incredible grace and courage by looking inside themselves and admitting that, yes, they too have acted in ways that may have contributed to the problem.

by **Rachel**

Third grade.

She was tall.

Mostly I remember her essence: pale, tall, hair that was thick and almost white. She wore light straight-legged jeans and loose t-shirts and had thick glasses with purple and turquoise speckled rims. She spoke gently. She smiled.

I don't have something particular to say. There isn't a specific moment.

I see her standing in the line with her backpack on as we lined up to go to gifted class. She came to my house once to work on a project – I see us leaning over papers in my sister's room.

I see myself dreading her coming. I see myself with an overwhelming dread, aversion, feeling of disgust for her presence.

There wasn't any reason. Except that she didn't play by the rules.

She wasn't the right size, the right shape, she didn't have the right clothes or talk in a certain way.

I had just switched schools and the rules were very important to me then.

I wrote about my feelings for her in my childhood journal. I went back and I wrote about her again more recently.

I apologized. I told her that she was perfect then. I told her that elementary school is a hard time. I told her I was sorry. I told her that her pale hair was beautiful and that her essence was kind.

I told myself, my child self, that I didn't have to be so scared.

I hope my actions didn't hurt her too much.
I hope she knows her worth.
I hope she feels strong, confident, capable of speaking.
I hope she feels empowered in who she is.

by **Leah N.**

Dear girl at the luau,

First, I want to apologize. I wasn't kind that day. What I should have done is alerted you that the world could see your backside.

I had no problem with the length of your skirt. Yes, it gets hot in Honolulu. But I was astonished that someone could walk around not knowing her behind was on display.

> **#YesAllWomen**
> because I work in a women's maximum security prison where hundreds of women have killed their abusers.
>
> *@misssaraatrspt*

I am sorry that your friend didn't see fit to tell you that your backside was showing. Neither did the other 300 people at that luau.

Sure, you might say we are all responsible for ourselves. But I have always appreciated when someone has told me that I have spinach in my teeth or when my skirt is tucked into my tights. And I should have given you that.

It was pretty easy to snicker with my friends, particularly since you were flirting with people that day. I didn't know how to react. It's really not an excuse. I just want to tell you what happened that day.

> **#** I had to explain to my 13 year old girls that the harassment they met with today will be a regular part of their lives from now on. **#YesAllWomen**
>
> *@youstinatinaa*

In Hawaii, they think things like sex and bums are funny. I know that is why they pulled you onto the stage. I could tell that da kine thought your bum was pretty darn funny. To get you onstage was nothing personal, just the natural exuberance of the people.

I knew it would happen, and I didn't say anything to you then.

You seemed so proud to be on stage. Proud that the cute Hawaiian men had picked you to come up and dance. You didn't understand why everyone was laughing. Being elevated on the stage put your bum on display even more clearly.

I really wish I had said something to you.

I could give you some excuses. I could say that you should have left your bathing suit bottoms on. I could tell you that I was suffering daily migraines, and sometimes, even without the headache, my filter disappears. But those are all excuses, and they won't make what happened better.

Unfortunately what I was thinking came out at top volume. "Nice ass!" I yelled. I admit, it got a great reaction from the crowd.

And sometimes I still find myself laughing. But mostly, I find myself feeling ashamed. As women, we get enough from male strangers. You didn't need it from a woman too. It wasn't too much to ask that I let you know that you were showing more than you had intended. And to say it to you privately.

I wish I had seen you as a sister – someone deserving of my kindness. I cannot excuse that I didn't. I hope you just turned red in the face and didn't take that moment home and cry. I hope you are able to find humor in the memory. But I don't know you, and I know it may be a painful memory.

It wasn't fair for me to assume that you would emerge unscathed and unscarred from our encounter. I have no idea who you were. I don't know what you were doing there and where life has taken you.

> #
>
> **#YesAllWomen** have been taught to make themselves look perfect but when doing so they get judged or slut shamed for it.
>
> *@Lirryhaze*

I can only apologize here and hope that you can find peace with that day.

As you can probably tell, I still feel conflicted over the memory. I feel guilty and have a lot of regret.

But sometimes it still makes me giggle – and that is what I fear about myself.

by **Crysti**

This is embarrassing to admit, but it immediately came to mind when I saw the writing prompt.

We've lived in our neighborhood for about 10 years. It's an old neighborhood with very little turnover of neighbors. There isn't a homeowner's association, but everyone keeps it pretty clean.

We used to have curbside trash pick-up that would take anything – and I do mean anything – very quickly. Recently there has been a population explosion, and the city has put more rules in place about what they will and will not pick up.

One week my family put some old carpet on the side of the road. We planned to haul it away if the city didn't pick it up that week.

A new lady had moved in nearby and she came knocking on our door, all angry that we had put carpet out. She never said hello or introduced herself. She just demanded as if she were the neighborhood association committee.

She must have just returned from the gym and was in short biker shorts and a sports bra.

It's amazing to me. I didn't grow up that way or think that way most of my life, but I automatically threw this slut-shaming bomb to get what I wanted.

Crysti

Instead of being rational, I yelled at her for coming to my door dressed "half-naked." I told her I had three young boys, and they didn't need to see her walking around half-naked. If she wanted a neighborhood association, she had a billion neighborhoods to choose from, but we weren't one of them. And if she had something else to say, she should come fully clothed next time.

> **#YesAllWomen**
> because my eight year old cousin got sent home for her tank top being "too revealing." SHE IS 8!
>
> *Name withheld by request*

It's been a couple of years, and she hasn't come back.

I hadn't even thought of her until I started writing this.

It's amazing to me. I didn't grow up that way or think that way most of my life, but I automatically threw this slut-shaming bomb to get what I wanted.

It reminds me of the law firm culture I used to work in. Women were often blamed for office "romances" starting or ending by the way they dressed.

Maybe it is ingrained in all of us, no matter how open-minded we think we are most of the time.

Ugh. How embarrassing.

I should probably bake something and go find out which house that lady lives in and apologize.

It is almost harder to explain to women than to men why we shouldn't make judgments based on how someone is dressed.

by **Mercedes**

The word "bitch" is extremely offensive to me when a man says it, even if it is used in humor. In fact, many cuss words are if they are uttered to me by a male. I make a point to let my male friends know when they cross the line. I suppose I make a point of demanding this form of respect. Interestingly, the B word isn't nearly as offensive when a woman says it to me.

I do not think that there is anything wrong with holding this standard. Perhaps it can be related to the verbal abuse I received from my father as a child. Even then, I remember letting my voice be heard and demanding respect.

> #
>
> Behind the **#YesAllWomen** tag, there is real tragedy and real pain. But there is also real hope & real courage. And hope & courage = progress.
>
> *@pari_passu*

There is power in words, and if someone hears something negative enough times, they eventually believe it or become labeled by it.

Is it wrong that I hold men to high standards? Is it wrong to demand equality between the two genders and how we treat one another? If society tells me that I should honor a man, he should prove to me that he is worthy of the honor.

by **Grace**

I live in Hawaii. It gets hot. It rarely rains.

I often spent time in a little tourist town hanging out at a café with outdoor tables facing the ocean. It's a great place for tourists to come and enjoy the beautiful scenery.

To see a man dressed in full leather S&M gear with a full hooded mask and high heels was completely unexpected. I could not understand why anyone would choose to wear that in private, much less in public. Much less in the heat of the day in a small, relatively conservative and religious town.

I remember wanting to ask him why he desired to be seen this way. I wondered what his personal and emotional life were like. Did he like himself? Did he love himself? Did he want attention…either positive or negative?

I thought he must have low self esteem. I worried for him a bit, because of how cruel people can be. I was very uncomfortable with his outfit. I wanted to ask him to limit himself to where I thought it was appropriate for him to "dress up" – at a club, at night, in private.

I just wanted him to disappear so that I didn't have to deal with the feelings he was bringing up in me.

by **Sabrinna**

This is hard to own, but I do judge the younger generation of women for their Friday and Saturday evening attire, and I struggle with this judgment. I hear them on the internet saying, 'I have the right to dress as I please', and to an extent, I agree. I agree that they don't deserve any kind of sexual harassment for how they dress.

But the truth is, I still judge them.

The saying 'I don't want to see what you had for breakfast' is true. I don't.

I also think, 'for goodness sake, exercise some class.' It looks so nasty when a young woman is drunk and on 6 inch heels or higher, unable to stand or walk, with everything hanging out of her clothing, because her clothes are so small they barely cover anything.

> Because school dress code teaches young girls that if a boy can't focus on school it's the girl's fault. **#YesAllWomen**
>
> *@Isabelx_*

My biggest problem with it is the lack of dignity. They don't seem to respect themselves as anything more than sex objects. They're emulating stars like Rihanna and Miley Cyrus. They're turning the Playboy Bunny into a sign of empowerment, when it's as un-empowered as one can get. It's playing into the male fantasy of woman-as-object, woman-as-sexual-gratification.

Part of me wants to scream at them, 'Wake up! You are not your breasts. You are not your thighs. You are not your booty.'

I talked with a young woman of 23 who had tried to hang herself. She was upset by never having had a boyfriend. She went on dating sites and hooked up with men several times a week. 'Hook-up' is code for meet and have sex. She'd been doing this since she was 19.

I tried talking to her about self-respect, that she's worth more than sex.

She told me she liked sex.

I said, that's fine. Many women like sex. The problem is when the sex doesn't satisfy the real need for human connection. There's a difference between immediate gratification that leaves you feeling empty afterwards and experiencing true connection. This takes time. It means holding back long enough to get to know the guy, to learn if it's a real connection or just a passing desire, lust.

She didn't want to see the connection between the depression and emptiness she was experiencing with the casual sex she was choosing. I hope things change for her.

Yes, a woman has the right to dress as she pleases. But why are young women dressing in a highly sexualized manner within an extremely narrow framework? Why is this sexualization getting younger and younger? Why aren't these questions being asked?

#YesAllWomen because church leaders seemed more eager for me to forgive my abuser than to confront him about his abuse.

@kristinwarwick

CHAPTER 17

Drawing boundaries

A mother may always put her kids' needs before her own, making sure that they get to all 12 of their after-school activities, without taking the time to have lunch with her friends. A woman in the "sandwich generation" may be constantly torn between caring for her parents and caring for her children, while forgetting to schedule her own dental appointment.

For many women, creating healthy and appropriate boundaries is a challenge. As natural caretakers, we often forget that the person we need to take care of first is ourselves, lest we run out of energy to care for others.

One of my favorite teachers, Iyanla Vanzant, often says, "You can't have a strong 'yes' until you have a strong 'no.'" We cannot truly go after and accept what we want until we are clear about saying 'no' to the things that we don't want – whether it's a job, a social outing, or a relationship. It all starts with learning how to draw healthy boundaries.

And the better we get at drawing and maintaining our boundaries, the easier it will be to surround ourselves with people who respect them.

by **Leah N.**

I've gotten better at drawing boundaries as I get older and gain more experience. I wasn't always so good at it.

As a teen, I could not understand people who stayed within their own lines. To me, living felt like something that must be explored. I wanted to push the envelope.

As the hormones subsided, I began drawing my own lines. This has been a journey of self-discovery for me. Where do I fall on issues? What is an okay thing for me? For others? For the world? I understand boundaries in my life in terms of respect. There are people who are allowed inside the lines, and there are graduating circles of lines defining the widening set of boundaries that I have in place.

There are some people who have drastically different ideas of where appropriate boundaries should lie. I have very little tolerance these days for people who cross my boundaries. It is disrespectful. It gets harder to hold my tongue or to keep the peace when people lack the self-awareness to respect the boundaries that have been defined either by society or an individual.

> #
> **#YesAllWomen**
> Because a single woman shouldn't be afraid to enjoy sex without being called a slut.
> *@cynthia_parten*

In this way, I am turning into my grandmother. That is something that will always bring a smile to my face. This woman was made of backbone, and if that is something that I have inherited, I am incredibly grateful.

She was a kind woman, generous with her love and time, but she had a firm set of boundaries that she enforced. She loved to spend time alone in her cottage by the beach. She needed it to recharge from the requirements of being a professor's wife in a small town. She was fiercely protective and was the defender, guardian and leader of our family.

She was intelligent and funny and, even though she hated to cook, she always made sure everyone had something to eat.

When my grandparents lived in India, she was appalled and heartbroken by the rampant poverty. Emily, the woman who kept house for them, was poor. Her yearly salary was a few dollars and a new pair of shoes.

Grandma bought her family many pairs of shoes, got them medical care, and cared for them as best she could. Emily and my grandmother wrote to each other for many years. Grandma sent money to Emily's family until her death.

> #
>
> **#YesAllWomen**
> Because the more successful I am in my career, the more people assume I must have slept around to get there.
>
> *@XtinaHernandez*

This part of my grandmother wasn't something she publicized. Only those closest to her knew the lengths she went to when she was called to help. Her heart was as wide as the sky, but she had learned the trick of retreating inside of herself so that the world didn't drain her away.

It is this trick, the one of sheltering inside your own lines, that I am currently navigating. How to keep your heart whole enough to be of service, but not to close it off because it has been damaged by the actions of others. I have a real fear of both – either being bled dry by the brokenness of the world or hardening so that things no longer affect me. It is a balancing act and one that I have not yet mastered.

Drawing firm boundaries is definitely the first step.

Grace

I love deeply. I have difficulty letting go. And yet I don't truly and deeply love myself.

by **Grace**

I care deeply about the feelings and well-being of others. Sometimes that makes it challenging to have clear and healthy boundaries.

This is something I am struggling with…working on… felt I had come to terms with and then realized sadly how far there is to go…

I share openly and honestly, sometimes to a fault. Who can really handle knowing everyone's deepest truth?

I moved 6,000 miles away from my family because I didn't feel comfortable in the role that I felt stuck in. Years later, I am drawn back into that horrible feeling of the dynamics that didn't serve me before. I love each of them and yet, I don't feel my love is understood, recognized, felt or reciprocated.

I love deeply. I have difficulty letting go. And yet I don't truly and deeply love myself.

I am big-hearted, have difficulty making decisions, my confidence is low...and yet I am intelligent, creative, passionate, strong and resilient.

by **Mercedes**

Resilience of the tide

Take all of me and then throw me away
A rare blessing indeed
I'm not scared of being alone

My solace is my reflection
My joy in tempo with the air I breath
My friends crash like ceaseless waves
I stand amongst the shores
In the end, beneath the night's many eyes.

Stability in the pond
Grotesque and ceaseless breeding of vermin
So very pretty, until you wallow in the scum

I walk amongst time's sand
I stand alone, but I live above
With every wave's attack; push and pull
I survive. Unbreakable. Lonely until the next wave appears
Waiting for the final welcoming wave to pull me under
forever into the abyss.

CHAPTER 18

Teaching children

One person may not be able to change the world, but each of us can change what we model for our children.

It's not uncommon for me to have a conversation with a woman who feels she can't make a major change in her life – whether it's treating her body with more respect, leaving a dysfunctional workplace, or even leaving a marriage. When I say, "What would you want to say to your child if he or she were in this position?" she is filled with advice and wisdom. When I say, "What do you want your child to learn from watching you?" she discovers a completely different outlook on the situation.

> # **#YesAllWomen**
> **because we are girls, ladies, women...not "bitches"**
>
> *@salzsalzsalz*

The old adage that kids will "hear what we say but repeat what we do" is true. They learn how to behave by watching us. They learn what acceptable treatment of a woman looks like within their family units, as well as what acceptable female behavior is.

A girl child who sees her mother treat herself with respect will learn to do likewise and accept nothing less from a boy and from the world. A boy child who sees his mother treat herself with respect will learn that is how women should be treated, and it will be natural for him to treat women this way.

The change starts within. We must be willing to make the positive changes for and within ourselves so that we can model better behavior for our children. It only takes one generation – one woman – to make a profound change.

We are that generation.

We are that woman.

by **Anne**

Sometimes I think my son does not respect me.

He has a friend who I see as a bad influence. I've seen texts and Facebook messages from this boy that were extremely crude, lewd, sarcastic and almost bullying.

I learned that he doesn't live with his mother, and that his father died a few years ago. I felt a glimmer of compassion for him. But I still didn't want my son hanging out with him. More recently, he convinced my son to go into a grocery store with him while he stole a bottle of wine. Later that night they were stopped by police.

I don't feel I can tell my son who he can and cannot spend time with, but I really have an adverse reaction to this boy.

I would like to say to him, "John, I don't know the circumstances of your father's death or the reason you do not live with your mother. I see a great deal of anger in you, which you seem to dull through self-medication. You often use harassment, sarcasm, heckling, and crude language and behavior to express yourself. I know you also

> How do I teach my son that women should be equal partners, but that equal does not mean the same? That they can be strong, have their own opinions and feelings and desires?
>
> ***Anne***

have a charming side, and a sense of humor that draws my son and others to you. I wonder how you feel about yourself, how you think others see you. Have you gone so far in your pranks and jibes to alienate any of your friends? You have a tough, cocky exterior, but I wonder if you respect yourself and feel good about how you treat others. I hope you realize as you get older that you can have stronger and closer relationships with others if you treat them kindly, respectfully, thoughtfully."

I've tried very hard to build a relationship with my son that is different from the one I had with my mother. But whether it's with this boy or not, sometimes his actions show that he doesn't respect others. Sometimes I wonder about the depth of his respect for me. That makes me sad. I worry about his apparent lack of respect, shown in little ways like ignoring his girlfriend when he's in a group.

How do I teach my son that women should be equal partners, but that equal does not mean they are the same as men? That they can be strong and should be allowed their own opinions and feelings and desires?

by **Crysti**

Respect is something I would like to teach girls…and

learn myself.

As a mother to boys, I'd love to teach boys to respect themselves as well.

I admit that sometimes it is hard to recognize this as a need. Especially for teen boys who put on a lot of bravado.

Today, my 17-year-old son left our shared computer on with his log in. His iMessage popped up. I looked and found he has been sexting two older women. We have talked about not sexting, having a healthy respect for sexuality, etc.

> **#YesAllWomen**
> because it's easier to evade unwanted advances than to say no, because they assume "no" = "try harder"
>
> *@haettinger*

It was disturbing to see him disrespecting them and them disrespecting him. I need to keep talking to him about respecting women.

After calming down for a few hours, I realized that I need to talk to him about respecting himself. And his long-time girlfriend.

I just wonder how to go about having the discussion. He is 17, and I know that all lectures fall on deaf ears.

I want to help him respect himself more in little ways. I think that part of the initiative to teach young men to respect women is to start with teaching boys to respect themselves.

by **Sabrinna**

This week I saw three different news items about attacks on elderly women. One was a woman in her late 60's who was beaten during a home invasion. The other two were both rapes of women in their 80's.

Unlike attacks on young women, they didn't reference drunkenness or what the women were wearing.

However, one report still had a blame-the-victim mentality. "What was she doing out by herself after dark?"

I have great difficulty with a blame-the-victim culture. However, that is the culture we live in.

I think we need a 3-pronged attack:

- Fight the culture.
- Teach boys and young men as part of changing the culture.
- Look at ways to minimize female risk.

> # Because if I am too drunk to drive home, I'm asking for it. And if you are too drunk to drive home, I'm asking for it. **#YesAllWomen**
>
> *@itsapineapple*

CHAPTER 19

Thinking about forgiveness

It has been said that holding onto anger is like drinking poison and expecting the other person to die.

On the other hand, anger can sometimes act as the driving force behind positive forward movement. Sometimes anger can help prop a person up when they might otherwise collapse in a heap.

There is no one right answer for every person or every situation. Here are some thoughts on the concept of forgiveness from the *You Are Not Alone* writers.

by **Crysti**

Forgiveness sounds so good. So honorable. So required.

But it's not. It requires people to say they are sorry. And mean it.

Then it requires the forgiver to be ready to accept the apology. If ever. If that person is never ready, then they should never be forced to give forgiveness.

I have heard over and over how much it hurts oneself not to forgive somebody. Holding onto a bitter root and all of that. I get that is a valid point.

But nobody is talking or making Pinterest quote pictures about how "forcing someone to forgive someone before they are ready is like assaulting that person all over again." I guess that is too long and doesn't go with a cute cat picture.

You can't give forgiveness until you are ready. And nobody should force anyone to do it before that moment.

> **#YesAllWomen**
> because women are told to forgive, forget and move on when a man abuses them and are seen as trouble makers when they can't.
>
> *@PoliceFailures*

by **Anne**

I was the primary caregiver for my father for several years. He lived in a retirement/assisted living community, so there was lots of help available, but I still shouldered a lot of responsibility – I took him to doctor appointments, ran errands, helped make healthcare decisions, made sure bills were paid, and so on.

As his health deteriorated, my sisters and I made a major decision – to encourage him to start hospice. He'd had multiple surgeries and had become very weak. He was unlikely to survive continued surgeries. He received the diagnosis of "failure to thrive." Despite that, he consistently refused hospice, saying he wasn't ready to die.

Finally surgeons advised no more surgeries, and I "convinced" my dad that it was time to go into hospice, to move "home" from the hospital.

Even after agreeing, he seemed to regret the decision. He said that's not what he wanted.

I often wish I had his forgiveness for persisting with the decision.

by **Grace**

I am in the process of forgiving myself for a life led in fear. Forgiving others for their inability to do as I would wish. And forgiving myself for wishing they would.

Forgiveness to oneself is the first thing one must do and then there is room for forgiving others. I keep trying to do it the other way around, and it hasn't been working very well.

by **Leah N.**

I hear a lot about forgiveness. Whether it is spoken of as a principle or ideal, forgiveness always seems to be associated with positive qualities in people.

Sometimes you hear about forgiveness in the sense that it is good for you. To forgive someone who has hurt you, victimized you or otherwise trespassed. I have felt intense pressure to forgive.

Maybe I'm simply stubborn. Maybe I truly don't get what everyone is talking about. I don't feel the need to forgive the people who have hurt me.

Mostly I have a good relationship with my parents these

days. I love them. They are good people, truly. Particularly compared to some people I know.

I wasn't abused by my family; I didn't live with a set of adults who had mental illness.

But when I hear friends speak about their parents and forgiving them, it is with the idea that these people did what they could with the tools they had. My parents didn't. They knew better.

I am more comfortable just moving on. I find more freedom in accepting what happened and moving forward with the situation.

by **Rachel**

I remember a moment in a movement class.

There were things I had been doing – specifically, acting inappropriately toward an ex-boyfriend, and I was feeling despair about it. As I moved my body, standing tall – perhaps walking gently or raising an arm – I felt a wave of complete forgiveness wash over me. I felt the understanding that I didn't know. Until that moment, I didn't know how to act better. I didn't know how to hold my boundaries when I encountered him randomly in a bar. And I couldn't know until I knew.

I understood as I stood in that wide room with wooden floors that I would have to learn slowly over time.

There was no one to blame.
There is no one to blame.
We are innocent.

MEN WHO ARE PART

#

If you're explaining to women how they feel instead of listening to them, you're part of the problem. **#YesAllWomen**

@Dreamweasel

#

Dear men: Go ahead and appreciate a woman's beauty, just don't assume she wants to hear about it when you're complete strangers. **#YesAllWomen**

@dean_garlick

#

When it comes down to it, **#YesAllWomen** is about a simple concept. That concept is human decency.

@BrBabblingBooks

#

I am skeptical, but if someone can give me a rational argument as to how **#YesAllWomen** and #feminism threatens men, I'll listen.

@Staticchicken

OF THE SOLUTION

If you love ANY woman, teach your boys to respect EVERY woman. Don't assume. Create good men by setting the example **#YesAllWomen**

@VagrantSays

Because getting a call from my sister after midnight makes me assume the worst. **#YesAllWomen**

@JMBoselli

Yes, it's not all men. The point is ALL women are subjected to heinous shit from men. We need to shut up now, and listen... **#YesAllWomen**

@TPF1138

As a guy, you can mock **#YesAllWomen** or realize that your fear of being raped in prison is what a woman may feel when jogging on a Tuesday.

@RealEdR

#

Because **#YesAllWomen** isn't just about healing women, it's about healing our society. It's about evolving as a species. #evolve

@StephieGilley

MOVING FORWARD

Acknowledging the problems of the past and the present is key to understanding where we are and how we got here.

Telling these stories in a place where they are honored and acknowledged can give us a sense of empowerment. But if we get stuck in the habit of retelling them, we can once again descend into a sense of futility. Instead, it's important to shift our focus to the future.

In this section, we focus on celebrating how far we've already come and how we can affect the change that we seek.

CHAPTER 20

Lighting the fire

by **Leah N.**

Today I spoke with a therapist and a pair of lawyers about the sexual harassment that I have been experiencing at work.

I dread going to the office. I have panic attacks and anxiety when I have to have meetings, alone, with the man who is causing the problems.

> #
>
> Because the Supreme Court says women aren't entitled to their own body parts when corporations are entitled to their own religion.
> **#YesAllWomen**
>
> *@bourbonface*

I've done all the right things. I reported it to his boss, and to human resources. I was told because his "intent wasn't malicious," they will monitor the situation. I was told that since I can't wipe the slate clean and pretend he hasn't made those comments, I must give this man the opportunity to change. That it is my problem.

And I realized today that this, for me, is the proverbial straw. I am so over this.

I am angry. I am sick and tired of putting up and shutting up. I'm tired of having to adjust my actions and words, having to monitor myself, because we allow men to think this is not only acceptable, but encouraged behavior.

> **#YesAllWomen**
> because a man can spout nasty comments about me and I'm expected to tolerate it because "boys will be boys."
>
> *@LindaAdamsVA*

It started at 11, and it hasn't stopped. I don't know what it's like to walk down the street alone and feel secure. How many times do I have to tell the same man to not touch me? I expect it at the bar. But in my workplace? To feel unsafe and unsupported and powerless is beyond aggravating.

I cannot accept that this is the way that I have to live.

I am done. No more will I let 20 years of harassment steal my voice and make me numb. I'm not going to let it go anymore. I need to relearn a lot – how to trust myself again. I need to learn how to deflect these men's actions back onto themselves. To make the perpetrators of this misogyny responsible for their own actions.

I'm sick of feeling like my womanhood is a handicap and that I have to work twice as hard for just as much. I shout twice as loud simply to be heard. This acceptance of violence and excusing of bad behavior because "boys will be boys" has got to stop.

Sadly, it was a woman who told me that my discomfort about the workplace harassment is now my problem. That felt like a slap in the face.

I feel like the dragon has been woken in me. If it's my problem now, I will handle it. But this woman is not going to like my fire. I am ready to burn this system down.

It is so good to feel flames of anger light within and to know that the passionate woman I am has not shrunk away.

#

It's been shocking & painful to remember all of these examples but I hope if we all contribute, it will end it once & for all. **#YesAllWomen**

@jennpal

CHAPTER 21

Claiming freedom

Women have come a long way. In the Western world, we have gained the right to vote, the right to drive, the right to enter the workforce, and the right to decide how many children we want to have.

> #
>
> **#YesAllWomen**
> **because people assume that if I take the time to put on makeup, it's because I want to impress a boy. Nah homie, I do this for me.**
>
> *@basareegajjar21*

Those rights have come to us thanks to the sacrifices of many women before us. They stood in the face of danger and disrepute to claim an equality of existence that they did not have.

Now it is our turn to stand and claim a new kind of freedom that we may pass down to our children. As women – and the men who stand with us – we are claiming the freedom to live a life without violence.

Let us now celebrate the beauty of who we are, all that we have accomplished, and our vision for the future.

by **Leah N.**

I don't know exactly what freedom feels like.
I am still tied by
words.

We are taught not to trust each other. We are removed from a network so we don't have the strength of numbers.

I am fighting to remove these constraints and become the woman I know deep inside – the one I don't let out to meet many people or to play very often.

I don't know what freedom feels like, but one day I hope to rediscover it.

> **#**
> Because people think **#YesAllWomen** is a fad rather than an effort to raise awareness for a real, current problem that affects everyone.
>
> *@BeKindTreadSoft*

by **Elizabeth**

Dear Person
  on the Internet.

Deciding on the words
to fit 140 characters
takes longer
than bullets.
More commitment
more courage,
thought,
happiness.

Don't be discouraged
when others plunge into violence
chest-beating rage.

Freedom-songs last
longer
than a trail of corpses
and broken
hearts.

by **Ashley**

"It's because I care," they say, "It's because you are unable to control yourself."

Freedom doesn't mean the right to take other's freedom.

Freedom of speech doesn't mean the right to a television show. Or to be heard. Or to give medical advice to those seeking healthcare.

Freedom of religion isn't the right to mandate what healthcare others seek.

Freedom means you have the right to practice and uphold your morals and ideals – and so does everybody else.

Freedom is for everyone, not just you.

That's not caring, it's manipulation.

Words have denotations and connotations. We have a responsibility to empathize with others and to ensure we don't contribute to the oppression of any group.

by **Elizabeth**

Words make meaning in a void.

Giving shape to those
who wouldn't have it
is hate.

Keep back up
straight
upright
uptight.

Brimming with
"proper,"
"malleable,"
"moldable."

I'm not your doll to position.

If you're offended
as I break down the walls,
pick up the pieces and build
new monuments
to decency,
propriety.

But don't be surprised when
they're dusty from disuse.
No one interested in kneeling
at their feet when freedom
is a frequently offered flavor.

If you know so well what should
be, speak your truths to the void
and perhaps your gods will help

build your world of clothed statues.

by **Mercedes**

Perception

Standing together, laughing at the irony of life
The night lights speak to us as they always have
Crashing waves of humble realization
Poetically eclipsed with the prospects of unity
Seeing as heaven could see, but never understanding

We alone keep this our modest secret
Veiled to the silent ears who have forsaken its beauty
Hidden from their judgment, we bask in our mystery
In violent fists and spiteful hearts they try to force conception
In silent comfort, we bask in its unfathomable splendor

In the crying rain and the closing of our eyes it makes itself known
In the clasped hands and tortured soul of a small child, it is born
In the forbidden embrace of young lovers, it lives
Together with the loss of a soul, it makes its departure

Realization mocks us, but always a painful smirk remains
We live unwanted but free
Our decisions shaping our spirits…
We love, we sing, we live…we stand…
Until the day's blind minds eventually come
Destroying our beauty of inspired reality
We, too, will lose the music of the night.

CHAPTER 22

Considering respect

In many ways this entire book is a meditation on respect: how much respect we give to others; how much respect we receive from others; and how much respect we give to ourselves.

Respect – or lack of it – is at the heart of every human communication. If we respect the other person, we are willing to listen, even if we disagree. If we don't respect the other person, there is no argument strong enough to make us truly listen and hear.

> # I really hope that my daughter will live in a world where her body is not the center of political debate. **#YesAllWomen**
>
> *@MEGACONNNN*
> *Meghan Concannon*

There are countless examples of this on the 24-hour news channels. There are the hosts who shout their guests down and the guests who shout each other down. It becomes impossible to hear *anyone*, because everyone is shouting and no one is listening.

We may not be able to change an entire culture with a few

pages on respect, but we can at least move the conversation in a positive direction – one where we speak up for our needs and agree to listen when others speak up for theirs.

> # When did rape become a form of flattery? Being raped is NOT a compliment. It's violence, hate, control. Nothing less. Idiots. **#YesAllWomen**
>
> *@Lurtle*

by **Rachel**

Respect is what I wish you had when you looked at me.

Respect my personhood.

Respect that I don't like being looked at in a certain way.

Respect that I have feelings.

Respect that I can laugh.

Respect that, right now, I don't want you to look at my body.

Respect that my body is mine.

Why do you think that when I'm on the street, my body become yours?

by **Mercedes**

When I see a woman who is on her own, much too intoxicated to make any sort of rational decision, or even stand for that matter, my inner mother comes out.

I am grateful that I have a strong sense of loyalty and am

surrounded by the same in my loved ones. We take care of one another in any situation, these ones included. So when I see a woman on her own in a foreign area surrounded by predators, all I can think of is, what decisions have you made to get you to this predicament, and worse, where are your friends? How can they leave you unprotected and alone here?

> # Because every time a woman gets pissed off at anyone or anything, people automatically assume she's on her period **#YesAllWomen**
>
> *@IHOPHemmings*

That being said, I hold a great deal of disdain for the men who take advantage of such women, or other men for that matter. It is nothing less than disgusting and appalling that such individuals do exist. I in no way condone the idea that a woman's attire or level of intoxication can be a justification for actions involving sexual assault of any kind. Our women should not alone be taught strategies to avoid rape. That will not solve the problem. Our men need to be taught to respect women at ALL times.

by **Leah C.**

This is my pledge to love…

I will trust you enough to tell you the truth as I know it in any given moment.

I will love you enough to respect myself; I will love myself enough to respect you.

I won't disappear without a word. If I need space or time, I will tell you.

When I fuck up – and I will – I will own up to it. I will offer explanations if they are necessary, but do my best to not make excuses.

I can't promise to not hurt you, just like you can't promise to not hurt me. We don't get to decide what another finds hurtful. But if you are hurt… I will listen. I might not be able to make it better – I might not even agree with what you say – but I will have enough honor and respect for you to listen to your feelings.

I don't want to mother you. I do want to help you feel loved, supported, and nurtured.

I will remind myself that you are not my father, my mother, my ex-boyfriend, my teacher…or anyone else from my past. I will strive to see YOU as YOU. And when I forget – and I will – I promise to reach out to my support system and ask them to pull me back to reality.

I hope that you will be an important part of my support system, but I promise that you won't be my ENTIRE support system.

I will allow you to support me and love me to the very best of your ability.

Leah C.

I will love you enough to respect myself; I will love myself enough to respect you.

I will support and love you to the very best of my ability.

When you give me a compliment, I will accept it. When I give you a compliment, I will mean it.

I will continue to do my inner work so that I can be the healthiest partner and the healthiest self possible.

I promise to laugh with you. *A lot.*

I promise to fight clean and fair. And to have fun making up.

I will remind myself that when we're at odds, I have a choice to be right or to be at peace.

I will endeavor to always see you as the whole and complicated person that you are – not perfect, but not broken; full of strengths and weaknesses; loved, loving, and lovable.

I will trust you enough to show you the whole and complicated person that I am – and not hide the parts that I've convinced myself aren't lovable.

And if a time comes that I can no longer keep these promises in good faith, I will strive to tell you the truth with love, and work together to find a way forward that leaves us both feeling whole and complete.

I have spent long enough without a partner to know what a treasure and privilege it is to find love. I promise to not take it – or you – for granted.

I don't know who you are yet, but I promise that I'm staying open to finding you. I hope you're doing the same.

CHAPTER 23

No longer waiting

by **Mercedes**

I remember looking outside my window as a child. My curls would dangle defiantly as I took comfort in the silence of the night. I would look upon the majesty of the moon and the stars making their way through the noise of the street lamps. Religiously, I would return there every night, and I would sit there waiting. Waiting for my dark knight.

> # The biggest obstacle you will face in life is drowning out the voice in your head that says you are not good enough. **#YesAllWomen**
>
> *@KATAuthor*

And that part is important. That part is significant. For a white knight could not comprehend the depth of what I was. A white knight wouldn't want to. A white knight would want a white princess. A white knight would ride past me without sparing a first glance. But my dark knight…my dark knight was there in the pitch with me. He would understand just how much I needed to be saved.

I would paint the features of his face in my mind. I would fall asleep with his image. He would be kind, mysterious, and appreciative. But most of all he would take me away, and I would be so grateful! He would take me to a new world. I would be given purpose, and we would be happy.

Years passed, and I still waited.
The screams downstairs would echo up to my room, and I still waited.
My body would be marked, but I still waited.
My eyes would be strained from the tears they shed, but I still waited.
Over and over again my heart would break, and the silly girl would sit there waiting.
Always patiently and devotedly waiting.
With the window open and perfume decorating my pillow.... I would wait.

I don't remember when the realization hit me...
Looking back, I don't think that it was by choice.
But the day came when my window stayed closed.
The day came when I realized a strange truth.
The day came when I opened the doors and left my metaphorical tower.
I escaped with nothing more than a new name and a new path before me.
For I was not a princess in need of rescue, I was a queen taking control of my own freedom.

I was my own dark knight.

CHAPTER 24

Choosing healing

by **Leah C.**

I've spoken publicly about the emotional abuse I experienced as a result of my father's alcoholism and how it has affected my life. But there's another piece of the story that's not so easy to talk about.

It's about how he interacted with me around sex. He incessantly "joked" that he would break the kneecaps of any boy who dared to touch me. He told he would lock me in my room until I was 30. I was terrified of being in a relationship with anyone because I thought he would hurt them and punish me.

While it was unsafe for me to be sexual with anyone else, it was my father who was sexual with me…he spoke to me sexually about my own body; he spoke to me about his sexual relationship with my mother; he spoke to me sexually about women other than my mother; and he spoke sexually to women other than my mother in front of me.

It took a long time for me to come to grips with the fact that this was, in fact, sexual abuse. It didn't include laying his hands on me sexually, but it was wildly inappropriate sexual contact with a child. In the years since, as I've learned more about this type of sexual abuse (which has a variety of names including emotional incest and emotional sexual abuse) I've learned that a lot of counselors and therapists consider it particularly insidious because there's nothing concrete for the child to point to and say, "That's when and how I was abused."

> #
> For those unable to speak, I lend you my voice. It wasn't your fault **#YesAllWomen** #AllMenCan
>
> *@Mama3Kat*

The child is left feeling like the one who is crazy. We carry the aftereffects of having been sexually violated without the actual event of having been molested.

I have felt this sense of debilitating confusion around sex since I can remember.

***

My entry into the world of sex came quite late. Between depression, fear, and a destructive self image, I was certain that no one would ever want to be with me.

Finally, at age 23, I entered my first serious relationship. It was deeply dysfunctional from day one. He was numbing out with marijuana multiple times a day, and I was so depressed that I couldn't see beyond my own nose. Neither us was capable of having a grown-up relationship.

When I thought about having sex with him for the first time, I wasn't anticipating something beautiful or meaningful...it was about "getting it over with" so I wouldn't be the oldest living virgin anymore.

It should be no surprise that with that attitude, it wasn't beautiful, meaningful, enjoyable, or satisfying. We stayed together for close to two years, and I cried when we had sex. Every. Single. Time.

I desperately wanted to have a good sexual experience, so I kept trying. I tried to bring creative new ideas that might help me/us, but nothing did.

At some point, he started telling me that I was broken. Specifically he said, "Your father broke you, and now it's my job to fix you." He told me that I wasn't good in bed.

Now, on top of feeling afraid and unsafe, I was broken and a bad lover too.

When I finally got the courage to walk away from that relationship, I was convinced that I was such a bad lover that no one would ever want to have sex with me.

***

Sex had become so fraught that I rarely engaged in it.

Over the next twelve years, I only had sex with two other men. In each case, I felt like I had to work extra hard to overcome how bad I was in bed, but I was also immobilized by fear.

I frequently initiated things, trying to be spontaneous and exciting, but once we got started, I would lie on my back and wait for it to be over.

Sex became something that I both craved and dreaded.

***

In 2011, after five years of conscious healing around my dad, men, and life in general, I met a kind, loving, and gentle man.

For the first time, I was able to be fully present.

Part of the difference was him. Never before had I felt so completely seen and adored for who I am, and that made it easier to show up.

But a big part of the difference was me. I had shifted my perspective to looking for the good instead of fixating on the bad. Until the day when he started to withdraw from me sexually.

It confirmed all of my worst fears. Not only did I feel rejected, but I felt like I'd been set up by the Universe. I'd gotten used to feeling worthless, and just when I began to feel like maybe I was okay, the whole thing came crashing down around me. Then he told me he wasn't in love with me anymore. It just added fuel to the fire of all those old beliefs.

Three years passed, and recently I met a guy. It was pretty clear that we weren't well suited for a romantic relationship, but we had great chemistry. I had to make a decision – listen to the voice that said, "I'm not the kind of girl who has sex outside a relationship"… or a new voice that said, "Why not?" I was ready to have some fun that wasn't so fraught with expectations.

A new side of myself was emerging – one who is willing to ask for what I want; one who is confident enough to believe that she deserves it; one who isn't willing to entertain disrespectful behavior.

And a fascinating dynamic developed with this guy – one in which I became the leader with someone who wanted to explore and wanted some guidance. The feedback I got from him didn't include anything about me being broken or bad in bed. In fact, he's vocally appreciative of our time together.

When I look inside myself, I see someone who is feeling stronger, more empowered, and more womanly.

***

And then, last week, I got a phone call that blew my mind. It was a message from that long-ago boyfriend who had told me I was so terribly broken. He asked if we could talk. We hadn't had a conversation in over a decade.

I have carried a huge amount of anger at him. I have been so angry that I made him into an ogre in my mind.

But as I anticipated our phone conversation, something big shifted. I realized just how much I contributed to the dysfunction of that relationship. I was convinced that I was damaged and broken, and I chose a partner who continually affirmed that for me. In fact, I couldn't have had a relationship with someone who treated me well because I didn't believe I deserved it. And because I believed that's all I deserved, I stayed – day after day after day, I chose to stay, even when I wanted to leave. For two years, I stayed.

> # Reading **#YesAllWomen** tweets makes me feel better and worse for the same reason – I'm not alone.
>
> *@ajiradarch*

He was responsible for his behavior, but he wasn't responsible for my decision to stay.

When we got on the phone, an astounding thing happened. We were able to reach back through the years and acknowledge each of our roles in that relationship and apologize to each other.

I spent a full weekend feeling like my head had exploded. How to reconcile twelve years of believing someone is the devil incarnate with a single conversation that shows that he's just a man who's been dealing with his own demons?

But it gets even more mind blowing….

> Being pro-chocolate doesn't mean I'm anti-vanilla. Being pro-woman doesn't mean I'm anti-male. **#YesAllWomen**
>
> *@IAmLeahCarey*

The next day I got another message from him. It read in part, "…even though our sex life was super dysfunctional, you were actually a very good lover because you cared, you tried, and you were adventurous. Those things were important to me, and I appreciated it."

Wow.

***

I based my beliefs about my safety in sexual situations on incomplete information from my dad.

I based my judgments of myself as a lover for the last 15 years on incomplete information from an old boyfriend.

And we all know that the largest sexual organ in the body – the one that governs our ability to feel and engage and respond – is our brain. My brain was so filled with incomplete information and other useless garbage that there wasn't room for healthy sexual encounters.

The fear of being broken and unlovable started very young and followed me through my life. Nobody is the bad guy in this story – I just used everything I heard from them to confirm what I already believed.

But it was compounded by the fact that I was too scared to talk about any of it. I kept quiet, so it festered.

I wish I could reach back to that 7-year-old girl, and the 12-year-old girl, and the 17-year-old girl, and the 23-year-old young woman, and all the rest and tell them – you are okay. There's nothing wrong. You are not broken. The only thing that needs to change is what you're thinking.

If you take one thing away from this story, I hope it's that no matter what your version of sexual fear/dysfunction/discomfort is, you are not broken. You are reliving some old messages, patterns, and beliefs that you picked up somewhere along the way...but you are entirely capable of releasing them. And you will when you're ready.

You are not alone.

We are not broken.

Men are not the enemy. Parents are not the enemy. Society and TV and magazines are not the enemy.

The enemy is this: SILENCE.

It's time to start talking about our sexuality. It's time to start sharing our fears and experiences. It's time to start supporting each other in finding our power and strength as women.

It's time to start being proud of our sexuality – not so that we can flaunt it in everyone else's face, but so that we can feel proud of who we are and how God made us. We are worthy of love and respect.

Because we are women and we matter.

> #
>
> I forgive you not because I became a saint, but because I am tired of hating. #forgiveness #PTSD **#YesAllWomen**
>
> *@altforgetful*

CHAPTER 25

Reclaiming our bodies

I remember my dad instructing me about dealing with menstrual cramps when I was a teenager. His words and tone suggested that he knew more about my body than I did. At the time I didn't have the courage to say what I was thinking: "Dad, next time you get your period, come talk to me. Until then, screw off!"

One of the challenges that comes up repeatedly in the #YesAllWomen conversation is the feeling that our bodies have been co-opted by others. People – both men and women – seem to think they have more of a right to our bodies than we do. Whether it's a man assuming our body is his to take, regardless of our consent, or whether it's a woman who feels she has the right to tell us when and how to appear in order to be "proper," it sometimes seems like we are ruled by everyone's whims but our own.

The first step in reclaiming our bodies is using them in ways that give us a sense of power and our own strength.

by **Ashley**

Throughout the summer, I faced taunts of "What if you get

muscley?"

The consensus amongst many teenage girls is that it would be better to refrain from exercise than to appear "masculine."

Or, in other words, healthy.

I decided to ignore these standards that others placed upon my body, and I trained for months.

Circus tryouts arrived, and I felt ready.

Pumped up by some Justin Timberlake, I walked in ready to kick butt.

I completed all of the requisites I needed to perform in the circus.

I felt powerful, as my body performed feats I would have been unable to do before.

I had grown strong both physically and emotionally. I was now able to surpass standards placed upon me by society.

Power is going after what you want, and overcoming obstacles to achieve your goals.

I felt powerful. I had grown strong both physically and emotionally. I was now able to surpass standards placed upon me by society.

Ashley

by **Leah N.**

I was grieving. I had lost my grandfather who was the most influential person in my life. I also had lost a three-and-a-half year relationship. I wasn't taking very good care of myself. I was living moment-to-moment, just enduring. There was no light at the end of the tunnel; the sun didn't come out for me.

> # **#YesAllWomen** is not shutting up despite the threats. The women here are showing bravery that should motivate all people.
>
> *@BrBabblingBooks*

I met someone who was a distraction. He was a terrible person. I didn't know that at first, but I didn't particularly care. He liked getting by on looks and macho charm. What he did or didn't do didn't bother me. The only thing that mattered was that we had chemistry.

He stayed at my place a lot. There was a lot of sex. But I didn't share a lot with him; certainly I gave him nothing of myself. I don't know what he wanted because I never asked.

I can look back and know that he was a deeply wounded person. He was searching for validation, and he was not getting it from me. I drove him insane, and it made him want me more. It made him want to hurt me, too.

We came back to my place. We hadn't been dating long. He really wanted me to love him, but I wouldn't say the words. He liked to feel powerful in bed. He wanted to dominate in every sexual encounter. I think that having the power to reduce a partner to nothing but her instincts was how he really fed his ego.

Usually, I'm okay with that. I am actually a pretty powerful person in my day-to-day life. It's nice to let go. But my life was spinning out of control. I was numb emotionally.

But that night an overwhelming sense of self and power surged as we were kissing.

I turned it around. I took control and flipped him onto his back. I controlled the rhythm and the touching. I pinned his arms over his head and we both reached a powerful climax. I don't remember having conscious thought of my actions.

> #
>
> Society lauds motherhood as the highest form of womanhood, then criticizes women for not losing that baby weight fast enough. **#YesAllWomen**
>
> *@pricharm*

It changed his entire way of looking at me. I think I frightened him. I made him feel powerless and out of control. And I think he liked it. But he was scared by the depth of his response. And my lack of emotion and response toward him made him angry.

That moment of power and the exchange of control framed our interactions in a new way, one that he had never experienced before.

For me it was a triumph – I felt more like a woman, and more in charge of my life than ever before. I let go completely – surrendered to the moment and the sensation, and it left me feeling recharged and connected to my body in a way that was totally new. It was certainly out of character for the relentless grief I had been living in.

I am still astonished that two people living the same experience can come away from it feeling so completely different. I felt re-seated in my body. I feel like that was the start of the way back to normalcy. That was a turning point in womanhood.

For him, it began a downward spiral of violence and acting out.

I see strength in vulnerability and in trusting someone. To allow another person the latitude to care for you – physically, emotionally or otherwise – is something deeply human. That shared experience can create a deep bond. I think that power is something two people can share.

He was not a man who could rejoice and enjoy a woman in control.

He couldn't forgive me for taking the power. He couldn't surrender. He never forgave himself for that moment. He never forgave me, either.

In the end, when he turned violent and vengeful, I think he was still searching for a way to take his power back. To claim my power was tantamount to stealing his.

by **Elizabeth**

After dark is hardest,
when the stories come on the TV –
news reactors
rapes,
murders,
flee.
Turn off the panic-box.

Set the window open and
imagine the peace bird in your skull
left
dormant, damaged.

Tell the truth this time
each revolution written in bones
carves a message that if you bleed
you deserve to do so freely.

Let the lessons of morality
stop carving our skin.

by **Crysti**

I live with chronic pain now, after having a tumor and a portion of my pelvis removed. I no longer feel powerful in my body.

Now there is a trade-off: no pain or no fog, physical exertions or mental clarity. I have to take pain medication even for a trip to Costco. I usually favor my mental abilities but in doing so, I am missing out on the physical world.

But when I was in middle school, I was a competitive swimmer and I did feel powerful in my body. My blond hair was crunchy and green, and I constantly smelled a bit too much like sunshine and chlorinated water.

The pool was my sanctuary. I qualified for the Junior Olympics in breaststroke.

I am not hand-eye coordinated and have never been very good at sports. But that day, my uncoordinated body, which usually had to work twice as hard on everything as the natural athletes, worked in sync with itself. It was a very powerful feeling.

I would love to swim again.

Just writing this makes me think nicer thoughts toward my body and makes me want to not hate it so much for its pain. To find a rhythm that will empower me to move freely. To once again enjoy sex despite having no feeling in that region of my body. To function as if I am fully alive, rather than already confined to a nursing home.

by **Anne**

When I was young, many of my friends took ballet or jazz dance classes, but not me. I was very self-conscious of my body. I never felt comfortable moving in public.

> #
>
> By the way it is regulated, you'd think a woman's body is deadlier than a gun #prochoice #HobbyLobby #WarOnWomen **#YesAllWomen**
>
> *@andrear54*

As I entered middle school, I would stay against the wall of the cafeteria during school dances. Even the one time I was invited to be a boy's date, I didn't dance.

In high school I avoided dances or, when I went, continued my back-against-the-wall strategy. I went to two proms and danced, but felt very awkward and uncomfortable each time. Thinking back on that time, I'm sure the discomfort was about low self-esteem, not liking the way my body looked, comparing myself unfavorably to other girls. In the locker room, I changed my clothes in a private shower stall rather than let others see my body.

It wasn't until I went to an all-women's college that I started feeling more comfortable with my body and began to enjoy dancing. We danced in groups, and it didn't matter whether or not there were any boys around. We danced for ourselves and no one else.

As an adult, I took a workshop in The Five Rhythms, also called ecstatic dance. After the workshop I joined a group in my community – men and women – who danced weekly, inspired by the format of The Five Rhythms.

It was extremely therapeutic and emotional – I found myself much more deeply in touch with my emotional core while dancing, and often cried or felt ecstatic. Others experienced the same.

> **#YesAllWomen**
> Because "Are you really going to eat that?" or "Should you be eating that?" is said to women while they eat. My body, my food.
>
> *@ASuehl*

The power I felt when dancing is difficult to describe. All of my body was connected…movement and feeling were intertwined. Heart trumped head. The other dancers supported, nurtured and contained my emotions, as I did theirs. It was freeing and glorious. I felt safe and strong. It was at times transcendent.

I was dancing with others, yet my focus was not all on them or their judgment (or, really, my perception of their judgment). My relationship to them was much more positive and open than in other dancing situations. I was open to their emotions – I listened with my body and connected when it felt right to support them.

Not only did I feel powerful in my body, I felt powerful as a person, very much a part of the group and giving power to the others as well as allowing my own power to shine.

by **Sabrinna**

I had experienced a horrible accident and spent three years learning to walk again.

I was visiting Christchurch for a few days and there was a festival on. I was going to go out with a friend, but he got called in to work. I decided to go out anyway.

I found my way to 'Midnight Madness.'

I got on the dance floor and danced in a large crowd of people. I lost self-consciousness and just allowed myself to enjoy dancing without fear.

At clubs, so often I've felt self-conscious, which has taken from the enjoyment. But this time I just felt like one of the crowd. I had a fantastic night that I would have missed out on if I'd been to afraid to go alone.

I felt powerful, not just in my body, but powerful as a person. My body was strong again and that was awesome. But more so, the powerful feeling came from not needing other people in order to do what I wanted. Also, not feeling beholden to the group. I could choose to stay where I was, go with people I knew, or leave early, no matter what anyone else was doing. I didn't need to negotiate it.

CHAPTER 26

Appreciating our sexuality

At the heart of the #YesAllWomen conversation is the radical notion that a woman should be able to decide when, where, and with whom to have sex...and that she should be able to enjoy it without guilt.

Why do I call it radical? Because that would be the natural assumption of anyone who spent a few minutes reading the hateful responses on social media to women's assertion of their rights under the #YesAllWomen hashtag.

Perhaps one of the most subversive actions a woman can take in the face of this is to truly enjoy her body during sex – to experience it as a vehicle for all types of physical pleasure.

by **Elizabeth**

Now
 just now
salt-bathed
universe in a droplet
under my tongue.

If I can taste your rainforests
I might not be lost.

I love when a thin layer of sweat
cools on me while I sleep until
4 in the afternoon, hungers sated.
When I can't find my way
to waking life, your touch is as
light as bird song.

You've helped me take my skin
back from the internet.

Just now
behind a blanket for a door,
a thin crowd outside, muffled in our
private corner.

You're on me, next to, around,
all the motion of stars cooled down.
The sun sets behind my eyes
after the blaze of a few dawns.

My love,
you have stars caught
in your hair and I can't seem
to come down from the mountain
top. The air is thinner up here,
and makes me gasp.
Crisp, a softness that cradles
bone.

I search your slopes when you sleep.

You held me before you touched me or
asked anything of me other than to share
a cluttered space in the universe. We've

made a pocket of puppets, gadgets, poetry,
and fantasy.

When we whisper what we want to one
another, we're building worlds.

I love drifting into an afternoon
with you, wondering if we had
only ever been supernovas, stars
slowing from our collision with
the pieces of our spirits and minds
left scattered as socks.

You've cooled the fire
with me. I've wrapped you in limbs
and heartstrings.

by **Rachel**

We both finished at the same time. He was lying on his back; I was on top of him. The sheets were tan and the walls were cream. There was a large wooden headboard at the top and the foot of his bed. Afterward we laughed, we poked at each other's bodies and pulled at each other's hairs.

> # I am most grateful for men everywhere that are supporting and sharing **#YesAllWomen** Thank you gentlemen for helping spread awareness
>
> *@KittyAndABook*

We recalled it sometimes. "Remember that time?" We both knew it had been good, when beside the same headboard something like that had long been caked in dust.

It's funny to be asked something positive about him, because the memories I hold, many of them, the ones I want to scream to the rooftops, to say that hurt, are of me falling down, collapsing. But tucked in between his dirty sheets are us laughing, something playful.

Now, I think, maybe there were lots of moments when we laughed. I scan the picnic table under the poinsettia tree, high school classrooms packed thirty desks full, my bed, his car, the park, Madrid, Vienna, Prague. And that one gem – laughter, lightness held between our two bodies as we holed up, stroking each other between walks, classes, parties, cars, lunches, conversations, books, glasses, palm trees outside his window, green Florida grass, his rough black driveway, and the tan sheets – stands tall.

by **Grace**

I don't remember how it actually started. I remember the "first kiss" as he pulled me toward him and began nibbling and kissing my neck. My back was to him, and the surprise made it all the more exciting. We were not going to cross that line, and then he crossed it and it was what I really wanted. The passion and hunger grew, it had been a long time for both of us since feeling that kind of attraction with someone.

I remember feeling extremely sexy, confident and free. I felt very powerful in my body. In my past I was often feeling unsure of what to do next or if what I was doing was good enough – if I was good enough – and with this person, that night, everything occurred completely naturally.

I was not only good enough. I was amazing. I felt beautiful, hot, enough. It was magic.

I had never felt a spiritual connection before. I had never felt energy move through me in the way that it did then. I actually felt a coming together in oneness.

by **Leah C.**

He didn't just look *at* me, he looked *into* me. He looked into my eyes and he touched my soul.

I had never experienced a look, a love, that powerful. I had never experienced the touch of a man's eyes that felt as real and tangible as the touch of his hands.

I could hear The Look in his voice as we fell in love connected by a telephone cord across thousands of miles.

I could smell The Look as the air crackled around us when he touched me for the first time.

I could feel The Look in every moment that we spent together, even when we were falling asleep in each other's arms, behind closed eyelids, sinking into dreams of each other.

And that first time – the moment when we first joined our bodies together as one – the orgasm started before the first touch. It started with The Look.

His eyes caressed my soul with such tender loving care before his hands even touched my body. And the girl who could barely muster an orgasm with other men discovered that it barely took a touch with him because it wasn't about his hands on my body. It was about his eyes on my soul.

This, my gentlemen friends, is what you have never been taught – you do not touch a woman with your hands. Not if you truly want to touch her. You touch her soul with your eyes.

This, my female friends, is what we deserve – to be seen, to be felt, to be known. When we find that space of communion with our lover – when we allow ourselves to be quiet and still, open and vulnerable enough to feel his love as he touches our soul – that is when sex becomes what we've always been told it should be.

That look took me to that joined place within myself and within him that had nothing to do with breasts or penises. It had everything to do with letting our souls lead our bodies.

Even now, three years since we last shared a touch, I can see The Look in pictures of us together. I can feel it when I close my eyes and think of him. And despite the pain of the ending, the memory of his Look still fills my soul.

That Look. It was everything. I will never settle for anything less.

#

Because all women deserve a partner who waits for an Enthusiastic "Yes" instead of a "Well She Didn't SAY No"
#YesAllWomen

@bloodlesscoup

CHAPTER 27

Finding community

So much of what we hear about communities of women is how catty, bitchy, and backstabbing they are. Some of the *You Are Not Alone* writers commented on those assumptions in their writing. At the end of our four weeks together, I asked the women to reflect on what they had learned about womanhood, community, and themselves during the process. Many of them remarked on how affirming and healing it was to share their stories with a group of women who were ready to listen. Even though they didn't know each other in advance, even though they're spread over the globe, they formed a community through the simple act of sharing.

by **Sabrinna**

I always felt some connection to women internationally, and talking within this group has solidified that even further. I didn't feel like I was talking to people from different countries. It felt like we all might have grown up and lived in the same place, walking distance from each other.

by **Crysti**

In this group of women I have learned that a community doesn't have to be wide to be deep. We were intentional about showing up and talking real. And it was incredible.

I have learned how diverse we are as women, yet how much we can relate to each other's strengths and fears. We may be diverse, but we can still hear each other when we talk.

I have felt judged over the past few years because I haven't been going to work in an office, so I didn't fit the mold of the submissive wife. But I am no longer going to stereotype all women as petty and judgy.

> # I think one of the most important take-aways from **#YesAllWomen** is simply this: you are not alone.
>
> *@mlvwrites*

In one of our early sessions, I wrote something about how women hate each other, how we judge each other. But not in this group and in this community. Maybe because of the boundaries of time and fertile listening. Maybe because of the caliber of women Leah draws to her.

by **Grace**

I was pleasantly surprised to experience an instant supportive sisterhood amongst the women that came together in this group each week. We are all so unique and extremely different, and yet a community was formed so beautifully. It gives me hope for this type of sharing and for building relationships in my future.

I didn't realize just how low my esteem had dropped, how intelligent and wise the younger generation of women are.

Thank you, ladies. It has been empowering and nurturing. And challenging!

by **Anne**

I was a little skeptical about how an online community could come together. Having been involved in a couple of women's groups, I thought the face-to-face in-person contact, rather than through a computer screen, was paramount. But I did feel connection with the other women and felt I'd like to know them better.

I loved hearing others' stories within this group. There was always something in each story that brought back a memory or feeling for me – there are so many shared experiences. It was comforting and exciting to hear the other women's voices.

> #
> Every day I see new women share their experiences here. I am glad they know they are not alone. **#YesAllWomen**
>
> *@ThinkHaddad*

There are so many different aspects of womanhood – the women were continually bringing up issues I hadn't considered in a long time, or sometimes ever.

I learned that my voice can be powerful!

I was reminded that I need to do this more often.

I realized that day-to-day conversations don't often afford

the opportunity to open fully and examine thoughtfully.

by **Ashley**

I have learned that I am not alone.

What once felt like a lonely journey that I was taking alone now feels like a mission.

The validation of my perspective is both hopeful and worrying. There are billions of other women that have faced the sexism I face every day, but at least there are others like me that want to change it.

by **Mercedes**

Women are beautiful in their strength. It is different when compared to the strength of men. I am not saying that one is superior, but there is a hidden beauty in the comparisons to be made.

During our time together in this group, we have been able to express ourselves together and grow from each other. Through these women, I have reconfirmed my own strengths, ambitions, adaptability, and my sense of power and empowerment.

Being present for the stories, talents, and amazing abilities of these women has been truly humbling and inspirational.

There needs to be more of this in the world. There needs to be more comfort and support provided amongst us women. Sisterhood is one of the most beautiful and powerful things this world has to offer.

by **Leah N.**

The support of this group of amazing, diverse and powerful women has come into my life at a time when I really needed it. To be able to unpack the events in my past and present and, more importantly, learn more about my reactions to everything on both a global and a personal scale has been invaluable.

I have learned so much about thoughtful womanhood. Not just a womanhood inherited from a broken system, but lived womanhood that has been identified, chosen, tested, and earned. The power in numbers and simple sharing can shed light on shared experience, and we are the narrative for the feminists who will come and take up the fight beside us.

I have felt the strength of the women in this group supporting me as I deal with my own battles. It is this shared power that has let me find my voice again and given me the spark to re-light my fire.

> **#**
>
> Shocked because I realized how much I recognize myself in most **#YesAllWomen** tweets.
>
> *@CleaSamson*

THE MAKING OF...

This section briefly discusses how this book came to be and how you can create your own writing group to explore these and other issues.

CHAPTER 28

Telling our stories

When I was growing up, my parents created an oral history kit called *The Heritage Project*. It included tapes for recording a loved one's story, along with a book filled with questions to start the conversation.

We have tapes of my grandfather talking about emigrating through Ellis Island and my great-grandfather talking about escaping the pogroms in Russia. They are priceless records of important lives. With that background, I was primed to believe in the importance and beauty of telling our own stories.

> **#YesAllWomen**
> because when I say "no," you shouldn't assume I secretly mean "convince me." "No" is not an invitation to negotiate.
>
> *@RachKenney*

For a long time, I dedicated myself to telling other people's stories. Specifically, I worked as a professional stage manager, supporting actors and directors as they brought other people's polished words to the stage.

I loved the theater, but eventually that type of storytelling felt a bit lacking to me. I began searching for a new way to tell stories.

In 2004, inspiration finally struck. I wanted to bypass the playwright and help people bring their own words and stories to the stage. There is a raw vulnerability that happens when a person tells a deeply meaningful personal story, and for an audience member, it is absolutely riveting.

That year, I worked with bestselling author Jodi Picoult to create and co-facilitate a writing-and-performance workshop for breast cancer survivors. Over twelve weeks, a group of eight women created *Bosom Buddies*, a deeply personal and moving exploration of diagnosis, treatment and recovery. We were invited to perform the show in venues around a tri-state area, our work was published in a medical journal, and we were featured extensively in local and regional media. I had found my calling.

> **#YesAllWomen**
> because I was required to sit thru an STD class to get a pap smear in college, while men could get an STD test without the class.
>
> *@Jaymeeson*

Over the intervening 10 years, I have replicated that workshop focusing on a range of topics with a variety of different groups, from female physicians to members at senior centers. Every time, the results are astonishing. People tell beautiful stories from their lives, and they tell them beautifully.

When the #YesAllWomen conversation began on Twitter, I immediately knew that I wanted to do a workshop about gender violence, but I didn't want to limit it to the people who were within driving distance. So I transitioned the workshop to an online space using video conferencing. That one change made a world of difference – literally. Women from around the world showed up to take part. The book you hold in your hands is the result.

We have lost touch with the beauty of telling our own stories. Inevitably, workshop participants tell me, "I have nothing interesting to say, and I'm a terrible writer." And then they start writing, and they create magic. It doesn't matter if they are accomplished writers or terrified at the prospect of facing a blank page. Part of what makes this workshop successful is that no one is ever left staring at a blank page, wondering what to write. We use writing prompts and timed writing periods that are short enough to encourage spontaneity and banish writers' block.

Many people are so used to not being heard in everyday life, it can be easier to simply not speak the important things. But when people enter a space where they know they will be listened to and heard in a deep way, they begin to speak amazing truths. That's what happens in these workshops.

When we watch television and movies – and yes, theater – we see stories that have been scripted by great storytellers. With a scriptwriter in the background creating perfectly dramatic situations and writing perfectly created dialogue, it's easy to think that, in comparison, our lives aren't interesting.

But here's the thing: long before television or radio or movies, there were stories. They were told through words and dance and songs around a campfire. They were the stories of the last great hunt, or the birth of the miracle baby, or that time when the great-grandfather fought off a bear. They were the stories of us.

Writing these stories has been a process of letting go and healing for the *You Are Not Alone* writers. I hope that reading them has helped you to realize that you are not alone. That very recognition can begin a process of letting go and healing for you as well.

You are important. You are worthy of being heard. And you have a very important story to tell.

CHAPTER 29

Want to start your own group?

To help you get your group started, a selection of the prompts that I used with the *You Are Not Alone* writers follows on the next page. You can use them as-is, or use them as a jumping-off point to write prompts that will be appropriate for your group.

If you choose to use these prompts and subsequently gather and publish your collected work, please let me know! I'd love to see what you create. Also please include a credit, "Inspired by the work of Leah Carey and the *You Are Not Alone* writers. More information can be found at www.LeahCarey.com."

Here are some suggestions for creating a successful writing group:

Choose a regular day and time to meet. You may also want to initially set a certain number of times to meet, and then extend if the group wants to continue.

Have a leader for each session – that person decides on which prompts to use, acts as the timekeeper, and facilitates the conversation.

Use prompts that are neutral and don't lead participants to a particular conclusion. Don't make assumptions that people will find certain words positive/negative, that they've had certain experiences, etc. For instance, one of the prompts I used with the *You Are Not Alone* writers read:

> *Write a letter to yourself at age 12 – just when your body was beginning to develop into womanhood. What do you want to say to yourself at that age?*

Notice that the prompt doesn't assume any particular positive or negative experience at that age. It simply suggests that there is probably a story to be told from that time in a person's life.

In order to get stories that have universal appeal, stay away from prompts that ask questions like, "What happened when..." That type of prompt will elicit a list of facts or dry details. We want more than a list of facts because we don't have an emotional experience when we listen to facts. We get emotionally involved in stories. Instead ask, "How did you feel when that happened? What did it make you think?" The details of each person's story will be different and potentially unrelatable, but the feelings that come up as the result of an experience are often universal.

The Writing Prompts

5 minute words:

Womanhood

Control

Fear

Respect

Freedom

Forgiveness

20 minute prompts:

If my friends *really* knew me, they would know…

Write a letter to yourself at age 12 – just when your body was beginning to develop into womanhood. What do you want to say to yourself at that age?

Tell us a story about a time when you felt like someone didn't listen to you. How did you feel? What did you need them to hear?

Write a letter to a person who acted inappropriately with you. How did you feel? What would you like to say to them now?

Tell us a story about a time when you judged another woman based on how she was dressed or her behavior. What did you think of her? What do you want to say to her?

Tell us a story about a time when you judged a man based on how he was dressed or his behavior. What did you think of him? What do you want to say to him?

Make a list of the things that you do consciously to prevent being harassed/assaulted.

Tell us a story about a time when you felt really powerful in your body.

Tell us about a time when you experienced really fulfilling sex. What made it special? How did it make you feel?

Think back over the last four weeks – what have you learned about community? About womanhood? About yourself?

Be part of the You Are Not Alone movement

Y - ***You* have a story to tell** - Visit www.LeahCarey.com and share your *You Are Not Alone* story!

A - **Amazon** - People want to read what others are reading. If this book helped you find hope and understanding, post a review at www.Amazon.com and help others to find this book.

N - **Newsletter** - Sign up for Leah's newsletter to receive notifications about upcoming workshops and books, as well as continued in-depth exploration of the ways in which YOU are not alone.

A - **Awareness** - Women are suffering in silence every day - at every age and across every social, racial, and economic bracket. Be aware of the women in your life who may need a listening ear and a shoulder to cry on. Help them to remember that THEY ARE NOT ALONE.

#

If Lucifer needs someone's consent to enter their body, then so do you! **#YesAllWomen**

@sofiaaeeriksson

ACKNOWLEDGMENTS

First and foremost, thank you to the *You Are Not Alone* writers who trusted themselves and me enough to take this journey together. I am so grateful to have met each and every one of you.

Thank you to all of the women who were brave enough to share their stories on Twitter using the **#YesAllWomen** hashtag and begin a powerful movement. Special thanks to those who allowed their words to be quoted in this book.

A book like this can only come together with a team of supporters, and I have been surrounded by the best.

Carrie Gendreau – for your continual encouragement and faith in me throughout this process.

Holli Harms, Meghen Hunter, Danielle Randall, Adele Traub – for being advance readers and wonderful sister-friends.

Lucas Cobb – for creating a cover that makes my heart sing.

Jason Robie – for helping me navigate the technical issues of getting the workshop moved to the online space.

Andrew McGregor – for technical help on every front and helping to keep me sane...even though I know you'll brush this off and say, "It was nothing." It was a lot of something.

Jodi Picoult and the Bosom Buddies – for taking the first journey with me 10 years ago. You will always be my first.

The home team – I could not do what I do without the mental, emotional, and spiritual support of an incredible group of mentors and friends. There aren't enough words of gratitude for Iyanla Vanzant, Nancy Yeates, Lois Paris-White, Ken and Renee Kizer, Judi Raiff and all of my Inner Visions sisters, Ellie Drew, Sue Miller...and so many more.

And finally, *Sybil Carey*. I was blessed to be born a writer. I was even more blessed to be born to a mother who is a professional editor, my biggest champion, and my best friend. Over the last year we have been through the highest of highs and the lowest of lows together, and we've managed to keep laughing through it all. There's no one else I would have chosen to take this journey with. I love you, Mom.

ABOUT THE CREATOR & FACILITATOR

Leah Carey got used to making the private public very early – she was on TV the first time when she was just 17 hours old!

Today, Leah is a journalist, transformational workshop leader, author, speaker, and life coach. Far from being born a natural optimist, Leah spent over two decades struggling with chronic depression. Now she delights in helping others to find the beauty and light within themselves.

She has been published in books, magazines, medical journals, and on many internet sites on a variety of self-empowerment and personal development topics. She also speaks frequently at groups and conferences on similar subjects. Her first book, *Transforming Your Body Image : A journey to loving your body* is a 40-day guided journaling experience that helps you to feel beautiful in the body you're in, rather than waiting to lose weight or get a nose job to feel pretty.

Leah lives in northern New Hampshire with her two parakeets, Cinnamon and Nutmeg, and about a bazillion of her favorite books.

> "Leah Carey is a bright light in the field of self-empowerment and writing as a healing art."
>
> **Iyanla Vanzant**
> *Host of "Iyanla, Fix My Life" on the Oprah Winfrey Network*

> "Leah Carey is a very talented visionary."
>
> **Jodi Picoult**
> *Bestselling novelist*

Want to do a workshop with Leah or have her to speak at your next event? Visit **www.LeahCarey.com** for her current listings and make a request for a workshop on a topic important to you.

While you're at the website, sign up for Leah's newsletter to learn about upcoming workshops, books, and to arrange a visit to your area.

You Are Not Alone

> #
> I think a lot of people assume the goal of **#YesAllWomen** is to persuade when really, it's just to explain what so many of us go through.
>
> *@vqnerdballs*

34738181R00103

Made in the USA
Middletown, DE
02 September 2016